LIVING WITH FLOWERS

REVISED AND UPDATED

LIVING
WITH
FLOWERS

J. Barry Ferguson with Tom Cowan
Foreword by David Rockefeller

Photography by Joseph Mehling
Additional Photography by Horst

RIZZOLI
NEW YORK

FOR DORA AND CHARLES

First published in the United States of America in 2000 by

RIZZOLI INTERNATIONAL PUBLICATIONS, INC.

300 Park Avenue South, New York, NY 10010

First edition 1990

Second edition 2000

ISBN 0-8478-2239-7

LC 00-130488

Designed by Lynne Yeamans

Frontispiece: Photograph by Horst

Printed and bound in Japan

Contents

Foreword

While I have never had a flair for arranging flowers myself, I always enjoy having beautiful flower arrangements in my home and greatly admire the talents of those gifted in this art. My wife, Peggy, always kept our homes filled with fresh flowers—from her own gardens whenever possible. Her taste ran to the special, seasonal flowers that she grew so well, such as peonies, roses, phlox, salvia, and delphinium. She always found the time to gather and arrange what the garden had to offer, naturally and without apparent effort.

Whenever we had a special anniversary to celebrate, Peggy would enjoy working with Barry Ferguson to produce spectacular floral decorations, which filled our house in Tarrytown and delighted all the family and guests.

Beside his work with parties and special events, Barry has another venue for his talents in New York City. For over twenty-seven years he has maintained the flowers and seasonal displays in Greenacre Park. A small treasure in our great city, the park resembles a country garden and was created by my late sister, Abby Mauzé, in the early 1970s.

I am pleased to have been given the chance to contribute this preface to a second edition of Barry's book, *Living with Flowers*. I feel sure the text will continue to enlighten generations of gardeners and flower lovers. The illustrations capture the vitality and variety of Barry's unique way with flowers and his enjoyment of the natural world. I am confident that readers, old and new, will understand and share my own pleasure in rediscovering this beautiful book.

—*David Rockefeller*

Preface to the Second Edition

In the years since I wrote *Living with Flowers*, the yellow magnolia "Elizabeth" has shot up to thirty-five feet, a trumpet vine "Madame Galen" has embraced a garden shed, and a tiny cutting of a variegated ivy, hustled through customs, has decided to take over a giant oak tree—that's the way with living things. Some favorite perennials have disappeared, others had to be banished, while hellebores have seeded themselves everywhere, thank you. Although some dear friends and treasured colleagues have left the garden, they leave behind fragrant memories and in some cases, a special primrose, a boxwood hedge, or a dwarf maple as a memento. With the initial publication of this book I soon found myself sharing my knowledge and love of flowers and gardening with new friends at botanical gardens and art museums from Rochester to New Orleans, Los Angeles to Seattle. The number of gardeners increases and today's modern nursery catalogs list rare and esoteric treasures from temperate South America and the flanks of the Himalaya, in addition to re-discovered natives. Impulses from garden extravaganzas in Europe and the famous English Chelsea and Hampton Court Flower Shows have stimulated our American shows. Seattle, San Francisco, Cincinnati, Atlanta, and Philadelphia, for example, host exhibitions that draw an international audience and showcase the newest impulses in garden design for desert or water meadow as well as the plants that are "hot." Currently hellebores, clivias in new color breakthroughs, hardy gingers, or weird "Jack in the Pulpit" occupy these places; passions run as high as the prices for wanted plants.

This second edition of *Living with Flowers* was encouraged last winter by Solveig Williams of Rizzoli, then the task was taken over by editor Ellen Hogan Elsen in association with publisher Marta Hallett, who feel as I do, that the text I wrote almost ten years ago is still valid—with some new pictures of course! My loyal photographer and friend Joseph Mehling jumped at the chance to resume our creative relationship and, with a new slant, has captured different flowers and fresh images to add to the text. A special word of thanks to my associate Tracy Vivona.

I am indebted to friends and neighbors Mrs. Joseph A. Thomas, Mrs. William Osborne, Mr. and Mrs. Alan Seligson, and Mrs. Margaret Howe, who have allowed me to shoot the new photographs in their homes, and I hope they have enjoyed the fun as much as I have. An important revision includes the redesign of the Care and Conditioning section at the end of this book. I hope you will find the ideas interesting and, most importantly, useful.

Finally I acknowledge with deep gratitude the kind words David Rockefeller offers in his foreword to this new edition of *Living with Flowers*.

—*J. Barry Ferguson*
Oyster Bay, NY
December 1999

THE
SEASONS
OF
THE
YEAR

LIVING WITH FLOWERS MEANS living with an acute awareness and appreciation of the seasons of the year. Flowers and seasons are almost inseparable. With the changes in temperature and length of days through winter, spring, summer, and fall, the year is a great wheel of color, form, fragrance, and excitement that is ever turning, always changing. The seasons keep us alert. They feed our minds and imaginations with new possibilities.

While the annual surge of life each spring is extraordinary and the fiery New England woods are intoxicating every autumn, I love and appreciate all the seasons, even the seemingly uneventful days of a long, gray winter, because for me flowers are the real calendar pages. They indicate the seasons sometimes far better than the printed calendar on the wall. And I don't mean just the cut flowers I have in my house. The flowers and foliage woven into patterns in my carpets, the floral design on my everyday china, and particularly the botanical prints and paintings that line my walls can lift my spirits and call to mind the varied growing seasons and diverse harvests in different parts of the world, regardless of how bleak the outdoors may look on a February day.

Winter

With the fall cleanup completed in the garden and the tender plants brought indoors, I discover my house all over again in winter. I lay down the big winter rugs for the living room and switch some pillow covers from the cool blues and greens of summer to the warmer shades of cranberry and aubergine. I enjoy both the labor and the pleasure of log fires—splitting wood, walking through the woods to gather kindling, and cozy conversations in front of a roaring blaze on a cold afternoon. For me, the smell of wood smoke on the chilly December air is a cheering winter bonus. I also get a chance to enjoy my library in winter as I search through

ABOVE: Even in the depth of winter we can enjoy the fragrance of spring with these blue and white Dutch hyacinths, lovingly presented in a wicker basket.

OPPOSITE: In the surprisingly bright winter light, spring bulbs will flourish for weeks. Ranunculus, though more complicated to force than other bulbs, are well worth the extra effort, and are available in a fantastic range of colors. In milder climates, these beauties can be grown outdoors in winter.

PRECEDING PAGES:
Photograph by Horst.

Gerard or Everett for the source of this herb or that perennial and discover whether it was Wilson or Farrer who brought this plant home from China or the Himalayas. In the world of books, flowers are always in full bloom and there I can indulge my unending fascination with growing things. My large collection of books on *Primula auricula*—a special friend of mine—keeps me in good company, so I am never lonely.

Even in winter I have breakfast with flowers. Maybe it's only a couple of red anemones in a glass against the frosty window, but they are a perfect start for even the dreariest February day. A few white tulips in the bedroom are great to wake up to—simple, perfect, and complete in themselves—and take my mind off the harsh weather waiting outside.

Flowers are always a pleasant distraction from the daily routines of winter, with its cold winds and short days. In fact, flowers indoors highlight what life there is outdoors, reminding us that there is life in the so-called death of the year. The resilient evergreen hollies and cypresses, the carpet of vinca, and the clumps of skimmia with their red

berries, draw attention to the subtle beauty of the otherwise bare landscape. Flowers by the window radiate with intensity in the uncommonly bright and searching winter light that peers through those windows it never reaches in summer when the sun is directly overhead. The slants of winter sunlight coming into rooms can make the indoor and outdoor colors play off one another in new and surprising ways, and a few late garden chrysanthemums saved from the frost, a Christmas poinsettia, or a pot of hyacinths can provide a cheerful accent.

For me, flowers are especially significant and assume greater responsibilities in the winter, when they have vanished from the garden. We value them more, just as we value the fewer hours of daylight. At a time of year when life centers so intensely on indoor comforts—fireplaces, books, soups and stews, cozy blankets, and woolen sweaters—we enjoy being reminded of the great outdoors by the flowers or plants that bring the expansiveness of nature into our tightly closed rooms. Our enjoyment of those few flowers may be keener as well in winter, for, I have come to believe, appreciation of their beauty is in inverse proportion to their availability.

In the leafless winter garden, one can suddenly appreciate the dignity and architecture of the bare trees, the pattern of limbs against the blue sky, and their shadows on the dried grass as the sun moves through the course of the day. I look out the window during these short days, mentally pruning limbs from trees or topping evergreens—an effortless exercise, but a useful and positive part of spring planning. Winter is the time to take stock of the garden, to plan the removal of dead limbs or spreading lower branches so more light can reach the woodland plantings. Consider spacing shrubs farther apart, even developing a mixed perennial border, an all-white garden or a bed of your favorite blue, gray, and lavender flowers and foliage against a screen of fully grown hemlock that now hides the neighbor's yard.

Winter is the time for dreams like these, fueled by the seed and nursery catalogs that arrive in the mail.

Living in a wooded area, I am aware that the outdoors in winter is never quite as still or lifeless as it seems. As the wind moves the bare branches, the birds that choose not to go south visit the bird feeders, hardy witnesses to survival. The house finches are in cheerful abundance, while the slate-colored junco pecks around to gobble the seed that falls on the ground. And the glorious cardinal, as red as the holly berries, is justification enough for putting out food during these cold months. Squirrels go about their nervous business, and I might even spy the fox slipping through the gray trunks of the trees. Suddenly an unexpected warm spell occurs and spring wants to make its presence known in mid-January. Tiny shoots of *Iris reticulata* pop up from the ground too soon, and I warn them, "Go back, go back." Soon the

PRECEDING PAGES: A planter box in a south-facing window is a place for a colorful interior garden year-round. Amaryllis, tulips, narcissus, and calla lilies, grown in pots placed inside the box, will thrive in winter.

ABOVE: A clump of snowdrops, lifted right out of the soil and planted with moss in a basket, can provide a dose of spring when the snow is still on the ground. When the flowers have faded, the clump can be set back in the ground.

FORCING
BULBS

No "force" is necessary in coaxing many spring flower bulbs to open indoors during the winter months. Daffodils, tulips, crocuses, and hyacinths can bloom, with just a few simple steps, to bring color, fragrance, and an early dose of spring to the house.

Paperwhites (*Narcissus tazzetta* family) are certainly the easiest to work with. A few bulbs can be anchored upright among small stones or pebbles in shallow water in a decorative low dish, such as the Chinese use. Set the container in a bright window, away from heat. Always choose plump bulbs and start with only a few at a time; keep the balance in a cool place. You can continue to plant them when the first "crop" fades, to have flowers through the darkest days.

Give a child a hyacinth to grow in a hyacinth glass, a vase popular since Victorian days. Most garden centers carry them. The glass will hold the bulb above so that roots can develop in the water below.

With all the rest of the spring favorites, forcing involves potting prime bulbs in clay pots or bulb pans. Plant as many bulbs as the container will hold in a loose mixture of two parts commercial potting soil, one part peat moss, and one part coarse sand. Make sure the bulbs' noses are at the top, just at soil level. After thorough watering, the containers should be brought to a cool dark cellar or closet,

and set on trays of sand. Hyacinths take approximately eight weeks to develop roots using this method; tulips and daffodils about ten to twelve weeks. If you can do it, the best way to develop a healthy root system is to give the bulbs a cold, dormant period underground. This is accomplished by digging a trench about 14 inches deep in a sheltered place or in a cold frame and setting bulb containers on a layer of sand or ash. Pack soil around the pots before covering up completely with peat moss or dried leaves. I would suggest also that before covering the bulbs you place a layer of hardware mesh above the containers in order to keep rodents away from the "tasty" bulbs.

With this method, bulbs that are going to be forced should be potted in September or October and examined in January or early February, when they can begin to be brought indoors. Bring in a few at a time, to a cool place where the temperature is in the 50s while the new top growth develops. The white shoots will soon turn a vigorous green and the buds will develop in a bright, cool window. At this point, I show off my trophies by setting the pots in a favorite urn, tureen, or basket.

For all forced-bulb plants, it is best to set them in a cool porch or room overnight or when you are away from the house. They will last that much longer.

Daffodils and tulips can be allowed to dry, then planted outdoors when the weather warms. Discard bulbs grown in water; their potential is now exhausted.

Amaryllis, always a crowd pleaser and available in luscious new colors, requires a pot merely one inch larger than its bulb. Pot the amaryllis bulb with just a bit of firmly packed soil, add water, and set it in a cool, dark place to encourage root growth. Do not water again until the flower bud thrusts through. Then bring it to the light, and the color will burst forth.

Left in the pot and fed a few times until summer when their leaves fade, plants—pots and all—should be set in a warm, dry place to "bake" through summer and fall. Toward the end of November, the amaryllis should be brought back to the cellar or cool closet, when, if you can believe it, the bulb is ready to repeat the process.

Why not experiment with some of the lesser-known varieties of bulbs and the fascinating miniatures, such as scilla, grape hyacinth, fritillaria, snowdrops, velthemia, or calla lily. Always choose the best-quality bulbs and pot them up promptly.

first primrose, eager to bloom, sends out an exploratory flower; a single crocus shows up on the sheltered side of the house; and although it's only March, we find that not just our thoughts but our feelings are outdoors after all.

I am always grateful for the local nurseries, the flower markets, and the intricate transportation network with its handlers and middle agents that can deliver boxes filled with instant spring to me from November through May. Even if it is just a token tulip or a pitcher filled with fragrant freesia, flowers are as important as orange juice and six-grain bread in my daily diet. The "best buys" during the winter months are miniature carnations, French tulips, alstroemeria (or Peruvian lilies), even certain spray chrysanthemums, chincherinchee, and the enormous variety of Asiatic lilies because they are long lasting and put up with a dry environment.

In general, our houses tend to overheat in the winter, and the dry atmosphere is not the best environment for household plants and flowers. I usually keep my thermostat set low (in the mid-60s) and run a humidifier to provide moisture in the air. The increased humidity makes the air feel warmer to the skin, so I can actually get by with a lower thermostat setting; and besides, I get to wear my favorite woolen sweaters.

I can supplement arrangements with forced bulbs and branches from the garden. From midwinter on, branches of forsythia, flowering quince, almond, or willow come indoors as inanimate sticks, but in the warm house and with persuasive loving care, soon they are anxious to burst their buds. I can also lift a few clumps of primroses with a trowel from among the dried leaves, set them in low clay pots, and put them in a cold frame. They then bloom weeks ahead of their appointed time, and are ready to bring into the house. I can also program an early performance from such easily forced spring bulbs as chionodoxa ("glory-of-the-snow"), crocuses, snowdrops, daffodils, tulips, and hyacinths. However, keeping plants in a cool spot is the best

way to make the blooms last longer. For example, set the pots on metal trays covered with fine gravel or pebbles on a window seat in the dining room or on well-lit windowsills, and keep them damp.

Because of their expense, flowers for winter parties need special care. Plan to purchase and condition them in advance of the event so they will open slowly and fully to look their best for the occasion. Keep the finished arrangement cool in the unheated attic, the spare bedroom with the window ajar, or out in the garage until it's needed. As long as the temperature stays in the 40s or 50s, the flowers will give a good performance at the party.

Don't overlook the possibilities of fragrant flowering plants that thrive during the shortest days of the year, such as, *Daphne odora*, *Jasmine polyanthum*, and *Chimonanthus fragrans* (winter sweet). These can be grown easily in pots outdoors during the summer and brought into a cool greenhouse or unheated porch after the first frost. They will gradually extend into bloom, bringing the great joy of their perfume to some special winter occasion. And speaking of fragrance,

I find that potpourri is a great help during the winter. Once the windows are closed for the season, and fireplace and kitchen smells linger in the air, a bowl of potpourri made from last summer's flowers can conjure up those warmer days and fresher scents. The "ghost of summer past" returns to greet us at Christmas or New Year's and brings to mind the color and fragrance of just a few months before.

Dried flowers from the previous summer also recall past months. The last few years have seen a tremendous revival of interest in dried flowers. Gathered throughout the summer, the flowers make a different yet traditional style of winter bouquet possible. Flowers that dry readily include hydrangeas, roses, honesty, larkspur, lavender, teasles, and stance; even giant cow parsley five to six feet high can capture the graphic forms of a season past. Although the fragrance is gone and the colors faded to muted tones, the shapes and textures of these old summer favorites can be a wonderful resource for arrangements, particularly for the country or weekend house, and remind us that no season is a world unto itself. The seasons of the year, like the seasons of life, overlap.

The time for reflection is over when the spring flower shows arrive in March. While there is little to do in the garden and it is still too early to plant, you can see what's new, stimulate your imagination, and get your juices going by visiting these traditional garden shows. No matter where you live, the sequence of spring flower shows can carry you through those last weeks of winter. It is a wonderful way to play the explorer vicariously—looking for new plants, ideas, and inspiration without any risk. The friendly competitive spirit among growers is contagious, and perhaps you'll want to accept the challenge to see how daring or colorful you can make your garden in the coming year. Just when you need it most, the spring flower show can fire you with keen anticipation, even if you only go to "smell the summer" while snow lies on the ground and the pond is frozen.

19

OPPOSITE: A visit to a public garden can fulfill your fantasies of spring while the weather is cold and the landscape barren. The spectacular conservatory at Wave Hill, Bronxville, New York, is a botanist's dream. Director of horticulture Marco Polo Stufano has gathered a collection of plants that makes each visit an educational experience as well as a pleasure.

ABOVE: The Palm House of the Enid Haupt Conservatory at the New York Botanical Gardens in the Bronx is a tropical paradise throughout the year, presenting flowers and plants the scale and rarity of which is unsurpassed.

Spring

Spring is the season of renewal, rebirth, and resurrection. The canopy of the forest starts to thicken and color as buds swell and the swaying willow dresses in a veil of bright green; the mornings are atwitter with bird songs; a shudder of anticipation sweeps across us at odd moments of the day. Everywhere we see surges of growth. Ice melts; pond water stirs; maples thrust out red and fuzzy flowers; the clematis suddenly has furry shoots; the house finch is making a nest in the vine over the door once again. The exhilaration of spring calls us outdoors to see, sniff, and touch. Like no other season, spring is a time to monitor, a time of frenetic activity for gardeners, flower lovers, and all outdoors people.

ABOVE: White tulips are placed with a bird's nest and quail eggs in a basket for a refreshing spring arrangement, framed with ivy and twigs of blueberry from the woods.

RIGHT: A dramatic arrangement is achieved in the early spring with forced branches of forsythia and white french tulips. Nearby, a pot of yellow daffodils and Narcissus "Cheerfulness" add their sunshine to the room.

FOLLOWING PAGE: An extravagant arrangement announces that spring has arrived. Included are forced witch hazel, pussy willow, and forsythia, Laura lilies, French tulips, Narcissus "Ice Follies," orange clivia, and double Evangeline tulips. The dark-colored foliage is *Lecothoe fontanesiana*, which is especially beautiful in early spring.

PRECEDING PAGE: In my own woodland garden, dogwood and pink trumpet daffodils speak of a new beginning. A fruitful spring garden is the payoff for all the pruning, planting, and cleanup performed the previous autumn.

ABOVE: A formal spring arrangement is a symphony in green and white. The forms of the green viburnum, Easter lilies, white French tulips, double Shasta daisies, and white waxflowers, with a touch of ivy, blend together harmoniously.

It is the season to prune the roses as the new buds break, cut back and prune the climbing vines and overbearing shrubs, fork through or rototill the vegetable and cutting garden, top-dress with a load of manure, divide and replant the crowded clumps of too-exuberant perennials, and start the early sweet peas. We wake up earlier just to take a walk while the air is fresh and enjoy the morning cup of coffee while we observe, savor, and dream.

In the temperate climate of New Zealand where I grew up, seasonal changes are gradual and subtle, and spring can begin with something as simple as the first camellia, that most handsome of the flowering shrubs. It is the classic winter-into-spring plant, beginning to bloom in the shortest days of midwinter. Its elegant leathery leaves and perfectly formed flowers of faultless texture are so varied that they

defy description—both double and single blooms in every shade, from white through pink to deepest red and wine with waved and overlapping petals. In the South, camellias are everywhere, but on Long Island they are difficult to grow outdoors. I am fortunate, however, to live near the greatest collection of camellias in the Northeast, the Conservatory of the William Coe Estate at Planting Fields Arboretum in Oyster Bay.

Early spring is also the time to bring potted auriculas from the cold frame where I hold them during the winter months and set them outdoors in a protected area to flower. These curious old-fashioned members of the primula family are also quite hardy and will bloom in the garden from April to mid-May in a sunny, well-drained spot. Like bordered pinks, hardy dwarf cyclamens, and the whole family of fritillaria, these antique flowers are among my favorite plants. Their enchantment only increases. Botanical terminology can change common names from time to time. Auricula are currently listed under the obscure name *Primula pubescens* and are available in a great variety under this heading. Those listed as *Alpine auricula* are the hardiest garden forms in a color range that includes wine, purple, rose, and yellow. The show varieties flaunt their more vivid red, gold, tan, and blue shades, each with a distinct and contrasting "eye."

The continued appearance of auriculas in botanical art through the ages indicates how much they have always been treasured. Especially in the seventeenth and eighteenth centuries, the modest auricula appears in the works of the great Flemish flower painters, just peeping out from the rim of the overladen urn somewhere between the damask roses and the double-flowered hyacinths. The smoky, muted, tapestry-like shades of these flowers can't compare with the luminous bright colors of today's primrose hybrids, and therein lies their attraction for me. As a result of two centuries of devoted breeding by fanciers and specialists, gray and green-edged varieties, dusted with powdery meal or farina, also occur, only adding to their elusive charm. The walls of one of my guest bedrooms are completely hung with pictures of auriculas, some rare prints dating from the 1700s, others painted recently by contemporary botanical artists. Like stamps and rare coins are to some people, auriculas are something I treasure.

In spring, as I drive Long Island's north-shore country roads, I see violets, winter aconites, and snowdrops coming up along the roadside. Soon the forsythia, which does better here than anyplace I've seen it, bursts into long graceful shoots of yellow as if it can't wait for warmer days. Eager daffodils, planted in the meadow in the chilly days of fall, suddenly fling their nodding stars across the fresh new green. The blue scilla spreads from under the bare beech trees out into the grass. I eagerly watch for the early dwarf rhododendrons to bloom and for the showy white helleborus to light up their shady nooks. I anticipate them all, and bring many of them indoors for a closer look.

An informal arrangement of tulips and lilacs in a Georgian glass vase strikes just the right note. Form is as important as color in combining flowers for a natural, unstudied look.

In Oyster Bay, the climax of the "spring parade" is achieved as the native dogwood open fully into bloom. Remarkable belts of showy white *Cornus florida* still exist through the woods here, and in mid-May I am surrounded by a veritable snowstorm of the papery white bracts on bare twigs. Aside from the exuberant Japanese cherry or vivid rhododendron in the Himalayan spring, I can think of no single species in nature that can outdo the elegant lacy perfection of this understated tree. Changing from lime green to creamy beige as the bracts develop, the color of the dogwood suddenly bursts into a dazzling white among the spring greens. The color mellows in two to three weeks to soft shades of pink, even green again, before the rush of leaves overtakes the fading flowers. A remarkable bonus with these desirable small trees is the second show during October when the flowers are replaced by clusters of brilliant red berries nestled among the changing leaves that range in color from red to purple wine—an ambrosia feast for the robins and grackle on their way south.

Because spring arrives so spontaneously, we tend to react with equal spontaneity. All the flowers of this season look so welcome and inviting that I gather them up in great quantities without feeling any obligation beyond the simplest arrangement. I'll use a sample of everything, in this season that promises everything. The springtime flowers simply want to be brought indoors before they fade. The subtle fragrance of each of the daffodil clan is irresistible, and who could ignore the perfume of grape hyacinths? Not to be picked but admired on the spot is the delicately fragrant trailing arbutus (*Epigaea repens*), happily thriving in the Long Island woods. Lily of the valley is one spring flower that demands to be picked in great bunches and enjoyed throughout the house in its brief moments on stage. Easy to grow anywhere, preferring moist shady areas with dappled light, the dainty white bells of "muguet de bois" offer their unique bouquet in early May.

Above all, spring is planting time, and as soon as the seed order arrives, we can think about the sequence of sowing. In very early spring, even in March, we can start the sweet peas, which grow best in cool days and flower in May and June, only to peter out by July. As I begin turning the earth for my cutting garden, I can already see the long rows teeming with zinnias, snapdragons, dahlias, salvia, and cosmos—flowers that thrive with cutting. For a reliable supply of fresh cut flowers, I usually plan a row or two of each variety, along with the token tomatoes, onions, beans, and parsley in the sunniest places.

In my ornamental perennial beds, I rely on the hardy standbys: sedum, astilbe, salvia, peonies, hollyhocks, summer phlox, black-eyed Susans, as well as alstromeria, foxglove, nepeta, and achillea in variety. They are all excellent cutting flowers and become staples of many summer displays. Between these old reliables, I may plant annuals such as nigella, or "love-in-a-mist," *Salvia farinacea*, and *Ammi majus*, lisianthus, lilies, new colored sunflowers, and a generous show of nasturtiums, Shirley poppies, and flowering tobacco. As the spring bulbs fade, it is important not to cut the foliage. Rather, let the leaves wither naturally to feed the bulbs for next year's bloom. If you don't like the untidy look, gather the leaves with a rubber band into a soft knot or braid, and let the annuals planted between grow up to conceal them.

OPPOSITE: The garden is the "face" of the house. People will be tempted to stop to admire this colorful and charming cottage garden.

ABOVE: These Estella Rijnveld parrot tulips—similar to the flowers said to have caused the "tulipomania" in seventeenth-century Holland—are pretty in the garden, but often have weak stems. They can be cut in bud and will open up inside the house quite sensationally.

The swelling tide of spring ushers in a garden show with varieties of iris, foxglove, and lupine amid clouds of dainty columbine. In the woods, the superbly blue mertensia or Virginia bluebell act as a subtle foil for late daffodil and Japanese primula.

The peonies respond as the days grow warmer and bring rave reviews. The large swelling buds of the tree peony open to shake out their luminous spring skirts of salmon, magenta, white, and an ultimate red made more intense and lustrous by the huge cluster of gold stamens poised within. I find it difficult to get much work done as they open—I have to check on them during the day, and usually cut examples of each to bring indoors so as not to waste a moment of their beauty. I will often keep several wrapped in tissue in the fridge to share with evening dinner guests so that they too can see this extravagant performance. As if their perfection of form, color, and texture were not enough, the tree peony is also blessed with a wonderful fragrance. On the threshold of summer the later-flowering herbaceous peony offers more of this exalted family and is a part of the early summer payoff for all our planning and garden work.

Flowering shrubs, on the other hand, often perform each season without any special fussing, and spring would not be spring without the fragrant abundance of lilac or viburnum, and the dynamic impact of the azalea in full throttle. While I prefer gradations of subtle colors, interplanted with complementary tulips and astilbes, and would aim to achieve this effect when designing or reworking a garden plan, I confess to the absolute bliss of finding the totally overgrown garden of some neglected house where azaleas of every raucous hue have grown to abandoned perfection for the too-brief, color-mad spring show. Azaleas do look their best growing freely rather than trimmed to cube or sphere shape as foundation planting, so give them enough room and group them by color. The brightest red or magenta are best planted in the open woods. The white and pale pink

ABOVE: Peonies are to be cherished. Their limited season makes them an especially valued flower. Here, a single red Chinese tree peony is displayed with some early roses, white Festiva Maxima peonies, bordered pinks, black parrot tulips, and dianthus.

RIGHT: Flowers needn't be arranged in a single vase. This spring grouping includes one vase of amaryllis and wax flower, another of lilac and Laura lilies, a vase each of mixed asters and tulips, and a spray of stargazer lily. One might vary the arrangement with the seasons.

varieties might best be placed under the *Magnolia stellata*, a distinguished small tree that is, with forsythia and *Cornus mas*, spring's harbinger.

From Nepal to Norway, from New Zealand to Long Island, something special happens, not only in the countryside, but in us each spring. I always feel like one of Chaucer's pilgrims who long to leave their closed-up homes and set out on journeys when the "sweet showers of April" arrive. A lifelong pilgrim, I want to be present and aware at that special moment in any climate or culture when it suddenly becomes spring. At that moment the spirit of place intoxicates all the senses, and the strength of the new season courses through the body like new blood.

BELOW: A nosegay of unexpectedly rich magenta, orange, and blue is created with lilies, cosmos, delphiniums, gerbera, stock, and eucalyptus foliage.

FOLLOWING PAGE: Summer's bounty of garden flowers brings fragrance and a country feeling into the house. Here, perennials such as Japanese anemones, Artemisia "Silver King," showy buddleia (butterfly bush), Lilium "Journey's End," and annuals such as white cosmos and cleome (spider flowers) are combined for a relaxed look. When cutting these flowers, make sure to keep the stems long; they can always be cut shorter if necessary when arranging.

Summer

When the leafy lanes of spring close up into thick green tunnels, we know that summer is at hand. The many shades of color that make spring a changing kaleidoscope of leaf and bud settle down into a comfortable conformity of deeper, richer greens. We find there is too much to do: we can't pick sweet peas fast enough, and all the vines need tying in place; the clumps of perennials need staking before the rain knocks them down, and we find aphids on the roses. Time to spray again. If you let it, the garden will easily take all your time. As this season of continual climaxes proceeds unrelentingly, I find myself wishing summer would just slow down so I could complete all of my plans, finish the mulching, catch up with the weeding, catch my breath, and have time to visit a few other gardens.

As the days of May lengthen into June, the rosebuds begin to form. I always celebrate the first rose of late spring (as much as mourn the last rose of summer), for with the roses come new fragrances. Reliable favorites among this "queen of flowers" are the climbing roses, for they are usually robust and bloom in great quantities. They are seen to best advantage against a house or garage, on a trellis, or over an archway or summer gazebo, but to encourage healthy growth and maximum bloom, the canes can be trained horizontally along a trellis or fence so that each node will send up another flowering shoot. Climbers may be the easiest roses to add to a garden design whenever you have sunny, open space against a fence or wall. The vigorous shrub roses, however, would be the best variety to include in a perennial border because once established they hold their own very well during the growing season and offer continued bloom.

The new hybrid tea roses are often scruffy, uneven-looking bushes after the first year. In this climate they often fall prey to every spot and blight. I often wonder if they are worth it for a couple of brief bursts of flower. But in New Zealand, in England, or on the Oregon or Maine coasts where the weather is cooler, they perform much better. Nonetheless, as a result of visits to recent Chelsea Flower Shows, I have fallen under the spell of the "new English roses" bred by David Austin and others. Some of these are

A natural touch is provided with flowers for a Manhattan terrace meal. Zinnias, Mexican sunflowers, and *Salvia coccinea* are just the right accompaniment for a cool lunch. Around the perimeter of the terrace, sun-loving plants such as lantana, hibiscus, geranium, ivy, and begonia can thrive in planter boxes.

totally captivating, possessing the charm and form of such old favorites as *Rosa gallica*, *Rosa centifolia*, and the Bourbon and Moss roses.

For me, roses must be fragrant. It's the natural complement to the fullness of their beauty. I prefer to grow those with a sweet perfume and usually avoid the hybrids bred over the years to produce larger or even brighter flowers but which have lost their wonderful fragrance in the process.

I am also partial to the offbeat, grayed colors—such as brown, lavender, and beige—with names like Brandy, Cafe Au Lait, Royal Tan, Butterscotch, and Sterling Silver. Their unexpected colors catch my eye; if they have a perfume as well, they are a special delight to arrange. Of course, the "red rose" will always be popular (I am reminded of Crimson Glory, Ena Harkness, and Etoile d'Holland in New Zealand gardens). And the vigorous, hardy yellow rose has universal appeal as its sunny countenance, highlighted by dark green leaves, reminds us in bold color what summer is all about: life lived to its fullest in the sunlight amid the robust green of nature herself.

Yes, roses need a lot of tender loving care: pruning, spraying, watering, feeding, even deadheading, but any true flower lover will find it worth the effort. After all, the rose in its infinite variety is unique in the world of flowers.

Care of flowers is critical during these hot, drier months, especially in regions not blessed with the cool, damp climate that makes English summer gardens so spectacular. We can appreciate the benefits of the mulched garden to conserve water and keep the plantings cooler and weed-free, and the wisdom of the soaker hose over the rotary spray.

With the summer harvest at hand, it is time to consider the annual display of such flowering shrubs as weigela, mock orange, deutzia, buddleia, and hydrangea. All are useful to cut for the house and can be used alone in simple arrangements or as the background for more ambitious combinations of all the border has to offer. Their generally cooler colors—whites, pale blues, mauves, and greens—are perfect to offset the hot and sultry days. Pastel tones and whites, like the light summer clothing we wear, contrast satisfyingly with the varied green foliages of hosta leaves, ornamental grasses, and trails of ivy.

For city and apartment dwellers, window boxes or tubs on the terrace or the fire escape can bring some much-needed color and vitality to the urban landscape. Whether you favor a profusion of petunias or verbena, begonias or lantana, or simple geraniums, summer is that much better with even a tiny garden to look after.

While each of us has favorites, most of us enjoy and appreciate the diversity of summer flowers, the exotic and unknown along with the most mundane. Sunflowers are a "must" each summer in my garden. In China, Italy, or Oyster Bay, this friendly American native has universal appeal, and seems to be known and valued in almost every culture. The great faces of sunflowers guarantee smiles no matter what language the gardener speaks. Birds love them for their nutritious seeds, and a painting by Van Gogh of simple sunflowers in southern France sells for millions of dollars. What other flower has so insinuated itself into our sense of what summer is all about?

Another summer favorite is the oleander, a native of the Mediterranean region, which reminds me of the highway medians in Italy. From Florence to Milan, along the Riviera too, these red, white, and pink flowering shrubs grace the roadside like exuberant wildflowers.

For twenty-five cents, a packet of morning glory seeds will bring days of enjoyment with very little effort. Because of their tough shells, it is best to nick the seed case first and then soak the seeds in warm water overnight to break their dormancy. As they grow, lead them up long bamboo whips to form a cone or bend them to create an archway. You can always place them among the climbing roses, or let them find their own tangled path in and out of fence slats.

Summer is the time to enjoy hydrangeas. The penetrating blues and pure whites that thrive on Nantucket always take my thoughts back to New Zealand, where the big-leaf forms flourish as ten-foot hedges. They seem to be part of every country view and a staple of every farmhouse. The lush flowers produced as pot plants here in the spring come in white, pink, red, and blue. With encouragement, they are worth trying in a sheltered spot in the garden. I grow and use the lacy white flowers of *Hydrangea paniculata* and the vast heads of the Peegee hydrangea (*H. Paniculata grandis*) in many summer arrangements.

In July and August I pinch back the chrysanthemums and the tall fall-blooming New England asters to delay flowering. They'll branch out and offer a greater bloom later in the season when the air is cooler. This simple treatment produces a greater abundance of flowers than letting them grow at full speed to bloom in the summer's heat.

Late summer is the time to take stock and reevaluate your garden. See what crop or variety proved successful, what planting or color scheme could be made more interesting next summer, and make resolutions about the layout of the garden for the following year. You may need to trim or remove a few trees to let in more light, plant screening hedges to provide privacy from new neighbors, thin out hedges along the drive, or decide that you really did plant too many tomatoes and could very well do with less next summer. Perhaps you should plant sunflowers or eggplant or kohlrabi instead.

And, of course, summer is the time for the great floral extravaganza of nature herself. I always enjoy traveling during these months just to see what nature and nature's caretakers are doing. The Old Westbury Gardens, Nantucket Island, the vigorous coast of Maine, and the green peace of Vermont where the growing season is so much shorter—

ABOVE: A fresh and lively focus for a room is treated on the fireplace mantel. None of the flowers used are spectacular in themselves, but together they make a dramatic statement. Included are hydrangea, cleome, scabious, blue lace flower, balloon flower, and roses.

FOLLOWING PAGE: Cosmos, in the garden or in a simple arrangement, are a summer favorite. They aren't complicated to arrange, as long as you're not stingy with them. In fact, they are almost self-arranging; the key is cutting them with varied stem lengths.

these are some of my favorite haunts. A New England summer is at its best when it comes to flowers. Here nature's recipe for growth and vitality is perfectly realized. There is water, sun, soil, and—most especially—the cool night air that lets the sap rise. In New England, the gentle sea or mountain breezes produce firm, healthy stems. The summer may be shorter here, but the seasons are perfectly defined.

But wherever you choose to wander in the summer months, there will be new treasures and unexpected garden surprises. We have spent enough time in our own environments during the rest of the year. During the summer we should see other habitats and flowers firsthand. Compare, for example, alpine flowers in Colorado with those in Innsbruck or in the mountain fields of Norway.

Most of all, summer is a time to enjoy ourselves. No elaborate or contrived arrangements are needed during the season of easy entertaining, whether we have a sit-down dinner party, a barbecue on the screened-in porch, or cocktails around the pool. Casual arrangements will perfectly complement the mood of a summer day or evening.

OPPOSITE: In the days before the first frost, dahlias excel, *Aster tartarica* tower over the border, and branches of Beautyberry (*Callicarpa bodneri*) make a joyful noise together in this simple stoneware jar.

OVERLEAF, LEFT: Golden Showers roses are an abundant bloomer throughout the season. Roses are worth the effort of growing, and bush, climbing, and shrub varieties can provide a ready supply of arranging materials. Instead of nipping them too neatly, let them go a little wild.

OVERLEAF, RIGHT: This summer dining table is a floral bonanza. Along with the design on the hand-painted English dishes, an oasis wreath of garden "snippets" on a silver tray is arranged with heads of Her Majesty roses, hydrangea, pink balloon flower, sprays of oregano, and leaves of prayer plant (*Maranta kerchoveana*). No "mean little florist's roses" here.

THE UNIVERSAL ROSE

The history of roses is filled with drama and romance. It is a fascinating tale that winds throughout the entire history of Western civilization. This universally loved flower, the flower of Venus, is celebrated endlessly by the poets and throughout literature from the Bible to Shakespeare to Gertrude Stein. It is the flower of kings, martyrs, crusaders, knights, and lovers the world over.

The old-fashioned specie roses from the fifteenth and sixteenth centuries are beautifully woven into Flemish tapestries, calling us back to another time and place. They remind me of the Crusaders who brought roses back with them from the Middle East to plant throughout Europe, not to mention the English War of the Roses, when the rival factions each had a red or white rose emblazoned on their shields. Many cities throughout the world have a rose as their emblem, and it is still to be found in the coats-of-arms of families of many nationalities.

And of course, the centuries-long love affair with this wonderful flower continues even today, as seen in the vitality of rose societies all over the world, composed of men and women who still take a passionate interest in this loveliest of old-fashioned flowers. We do well to honor the "queen of flowers," for it is usually one of the first, if not *the* first, flower we were all able to recognize—and love—as children.

Autumn

John Keats called it a "season of mists and mellow fruitfulness." And indeed it is a time of gentle, softer tones. Water vapor hangs in the air, and the muted, hazy landscapes have a dreamlike quality, especially in the early morning as the subtle hints of color glow through the woods. Like the other seasons, autumn has its own character; it is not just the end of the year. As the seasons change, there really are no final curtains coming down; each season is a new act, and although a favorite set may be moved offstage, another is waiting in the wings to be rolled out in its place. I've seen the

LEFT: The casual placement of flowers throughout the house has a welcoming effect. In this country kitchen, hybrid sunflowers are gathered in a low bowl with ripe berries of *Viburnum opulus* and ears of green barley on the old painted-pine cupboard. On the table is a small glass filled with yellow and orange cosmos.

ABOVE: From late September or early October until frost, dahlias exuberantly come forth. Their flowers should be cut to encourage new growth, so they are perfect for weeks of color indoors as well.

seasons around the world, and have fallen in love with autumns in many locales, but for me autumn in New England and the Northeast is the most spectacular.

The reds here have the greatest appeal: the flashing orange-red of dogwood berries nestled in the smoky rose and pink of their fall outfit; brilliant scarlet holly and skimmia berries glittering among the lustrous deep green leaves. After the first frost, I'm surprised at the brilliance of the winterberry, the native deciduous *Ilex verticillata*, luminous and totally captivating. The sourwood or sorrel tree, oxydendron, climbs through a range of reds as it builds to its fall climax from a deep mahogany to cream and scarlet. The sweet gum, or liquidambar, with its star-shaped leaves, makes an equally fine showing. But *Nyssa sylvatica*, the sour gum or black tupelo, wins hands down in the scarlet stakes if you are lucky enough to discover one standing at the edge of a pond or lake and reflected in the still water—always a bravura display if the lighting is right. Later in the season come the Japanese maples with a brilliance and clarity of color to make one gasp. They are lovely wherever they occur: in great drifts at the edge of the forest, alone in a suburban garden, or glimpsed through the mists of Lake Chuzenji in Japan, clinging to the rocky cliffs above Nikko in broken splashes of intoxicating color.

Autumn is truly the Wagnerian season trumpeting the grand entrance (and exit) of nature's most brilliant colors, the greatly anticipated climax when the year offers its last glorious gesture to delight the eye. In the woods of New England, from Vermont south, she gives us this wonderful burst of new energy right at the end, displayed in colors and patterns that transcend anything the human imagination could design. And all of a sudden my garden is colored with gold, rose, deep reds, and lavender.

Autumn is a relief after the busyness of summer and the wilting days of July and August. From mid-September until the first frost, plants we thought had bloomed their last take on new life. The asters I cut back in summer start to bud up again and show their colors; the black-eyed Susans have a wonderful reprieve in September and October, as do rose hips and crab apple. The hawthorne and euonymus color the roadside, while the roses are bigger and more colorful than in June. Even our window boxes look revived, as if (to borrow from Keats again) "they think warm days will never cease."

Lavender and larkspur are gathered for drying throughout the summer, along with rose petals for potpourri. But fall, the harvest season, is for gathering and bringing in: the seedheads of alliums, delphiniums, and lilies; the now-dried stalks of flowering plants, like teasel, and the flowering grasses, such as pennisetum, or fountain grass, and miscanthus. I collect them all before the winter storms destroy their beauty. Every day seems to threaten "last chance," yet I am delighted to find autumn lingering for yet another day, another weekend. I keep my spirits unattached and go with the drift of things, letting nature set the pace.

Many garden flowers are at their best in the "overtime" of Indian summer. Roses have deeper color and more fragrance, and cosmos, sunflowers, salvia, aconitum, Japanese anemones, and ornamental grasses enjoy this extended growing season. Many fruits are just coming into their full ripeness: apples, late raspberries, tomatoes, brown pears, and the black-purple Concord grapes that will fall from the vine if we don't snip them.

A simple arrangement of
annual Chinese asters
and buddleia is at home
in a purple glass vase.

For me, the late-blooming chrysanthemums in their many varieties have a most important role in the autumn garden. This delicate flower in different colors of the Korean hybrids survives in old gardens. A massed planting of them in New York's Central Park Conservatory garden on Fifth Avenue makes a visit there a delightful surprise in late October. They are as special as the first primrose in spring, the first rose in June, the wood smoke on a nippy October day.

As long as the weather holds, autumn is the time to wind up those last chores and get the garden ready for its winter rest. You may decide not to prune the forsythia so you can bring branches indoors to force during the winter, but do prune the grapevines to fashion into winter wreaths for the holidays. It is certainly time to pile the mulch high around the rosebushes when the frost has done its killing work, and leave them dormant until the growth pushes out next spring. Now is the time to plant all of the bulbs you ordered, naturalizing daffodils for the meadow or orchard, scilla and crocus for the border of the house, and a brave show of tulips for the beds in the front lawn. Tuck them well in, cover with mulched leaves, and let them sleep until spring.

I always find premonitions of the coming spring even in late fall: the amazing colchicum, or autumn crocus, dazzling and waxy in heliotrope and lavender, is especially lovely in its pure white form. Could it be a leftover of last spring, or a preview of the spring to come? The yellow, crocuslike *Sternbergia lutea* and fall cyclamen (*C. neapolitanum*) seem like a promise of April to me as I watch the seasons tumble into one another. The dried bird's nest, empty now high in the branches, is waiting for its occupants to return. And so I prepare for the winter days, confident that nature never disappoints us. Each season flows as it should, into the next, and the season around the corner is closer than we think.

A WREATH WITH GRAPEVINE

Grapes were growing in North America long before the first settlers arrived. The Viking explorer Leif Eriksson wrote around the year 1000, "I have found vines and grapes. I have named this land Vineland."

The vigorous climbing members of the vitis family (*V. labrusca*, the fox grape; *V. aestivalis*, the pigeon grape; and *V. rotunifolia*, or muscadine grape) are hardy New World natives that grow from the colder northern parts of New England all the way down to the central and southern states. The brown vines with thin ribbons of flaking bark and wispy tendrils can be woven into baskets or trays by weaving or twisting. However, the simplest shape is the wreath: a decorated circle of branches and flowers that may be as old as humankind. Grapevine wreaths are easily made by twining both the thick and thin strands of vine around themselves to make a vigorous, sturdy skein. I suggest a diameter of 24–30 inches and a generous thickness of 6–8 inches. Hide any loose ends by tucking them into the layers and use thin wire if necessary to control any wild shoots. I recommend a wire frame for wreaths more than 24 inches in diameter.

The basic wreath is always appropriate for harvest time and around Thanksgiving. It could be trimmed with a bird's nest; tiny bunches of dried herbs, flowers, or seed heads; or simple bows of raffia, burlap, or ribbon. Consider adding tiny lady apples, beechnuts in clusters, sprays of red holly berries, fresh cut evergreens, and a bright plaid bow to the wreath for the front door at Christmas.

SETTINGS

S
OMETHING ABOUT FLOWERS
growing in the open air and sunshine cries out
for my attention. I know that their timeless qualities of color, fragrance, and beauty will not last forever in
the garden or along the roadside. They deserve my attention,
and I always want to bring some home with me to enjoy
their transient beauty indoors. Here I can study their structure, watch them as they develop to maturity, and wonder at
their infinite variety of form and color. Like my daily dose
of Mozart, I need flowers around me.

More people today are bringing flowers in from the garden, the roadside, and the market. In the bag of groceries, next
to the stalk of celery or the loaf of French bread, I see bouquets of fresh flowers. The twenty-four-hour flower shops
and the flower sections in our grocery stores are playing an
important role in satisfying an appetite beyond food and
wine. Whatever the setting—where we chop potatoes, watch
television, brush our teeth, or spend time with family or
friends—flowers complement everything we do in a wonderfully nonintrusive way. They are forever enriching our lives.

I enjoy flowers and plants throughout the house year-
round, whether it's a great bouquet of dahlias or cosmos in
late summer, or a precious branch of forced forsythia in

RIGHT: Flowers should
blend into a roomscape, but
never "coordinate." In this
mixed-period room, where
Chippendale meets Dubuffet,
a group of long-stemmed
tulips is displayed in a
contemporary ceramic jar.

PRECEDING PAGES:
Photograph by Horst.

midwinter. Their life and vitality uplift me on the grayest days and mark the changing patterns of the seasons. I am constantly looking forward to the next batch, anticipating the seasons as we move through the year. But never a season goes by that I do not find the right flowers to bring into the spaces where I live and work.

Even in the long northern winter when the garden is empty and the trees are bare, I pamper myself with fresh flowers in my living spaces and in the office as well. They keep my spirits up. Yes, flowers do fade; but there is pleasure in watching the cycle of their growth: the forced daffodils coming into bloom, their very impermanence heightening their tremendous appeal; the first yellow narcissus poking up among the dry leaves of last fall; the first rosebud of June from the new climber. I want them all to stay, to last; I want to savor them a little longer. Living with a garden, however, makes the difference because you can control the supply and variety of flowers.

Flowers at Home

The degree to which we can involve flowers in our lives is a personal matter that depends, of course, on how and where we live. Not everyone is lucky enough to have access to wild country flowers that grow along roadsides and in fields. Nor does everyone have space for a simple garden. And the amount of space that can be committed to flowers indoors varies from household to household. Nevertheless, I don't know of a house or apartment where flowers would not be a welcome addition to a dining or side table, shelf, or window area.

In my home—a combination living area, office, and studio built in a renovated carriage house and stable—I have a freewheeling space for living, entertaining, and work. My North Shore garden is naturally crowded with things I can cut—roses and hellebores, peonies and asters, as well as the tomatoes, zinnias, herbs, and sunflowers. The pleasure of growing these old friends in sunny and woodland areas so

close to where I live and work makes me feel as if these outdoor flower arrangements are actually "in house," so to speak. While I depend on the New York flower market for my commercial work, I prefer to draw on the garden and local resources for as often and as long as possible for my house flowers.

To me, flowers have never been a luxury, reserved like champagne for special occasions, for the drawing room, or for when guests are expected. They are as necessary as fresh orange juice, classical music, and the telephone. A sparsely furnished one-room apartment in the city when you are just

PRECEDING PAGES, LEFT:
Snow covered the ground when I picked this winter bouquet in mid-February. Fragrant yellow *hamamelis* (or Chinese witchhazel), bright green flowers of *Helleborus foetidus,* and the gold stars of *Jasmin nudiflorum* shine against the leaves and flowers of dramatic Mahonia.

PRECEDING PAGES, RIGHT:
A surprise for winter luncheon guests: a collection of greenhouse camellia gathered among some of my favorite things.

ABOVE: A converted stable, the setting for a summer party, is spruced up with a bouquet of French Lace and Floribunda roses in a simple ceramic batter pitcher. Enough is enough—especially with roses.

starting out in life needs flowers as much as the suburban home, possibly more so. The beauty of an austere apartment is that it doesn't take many flowers to transform it because there is not much in it by way of competition. A wine carafe with a handful of yellow tulips, plus Vivaldi on the stereo, can make the space come alive with color and music. Bring out some cheese and wine, and your one-room apartment is ready for a party.

I am lucky to have grown up in a family that loved to garden and in a land where fruit, flowers, and vegetables grew so well. Among my childhood memories of New Zealand are the lavender wisteria and cerise bougainvillaea twined together over a balcony in Napier, blue poppies and candelabra primula in the shade of giant rhododendrons in Dunedin, cineraria seeding themselves to bloom in gaudy purple and magenta profusion in the shelter of vast hydrangea banks in Wellington, the golden gorse gone wild covering the hillside with its fragrance on warm days, and the unforgettable perfume of the yellow tree lupine on the sand hills around our beach cottage. Thank heavens I learned early about sowing radish and cress seeds and picking tomatoes and climbing the persimmon and loquat trees to help myself to their fruit. Among the things I am most grateful for in my youth was the encouragement I had from my family to gather flowers, weeds, and grasses for the vases in the house, for in these simple tasks and pleasures were sown the seeds of my later life. Growing up with flowers was quite natural, surrounded by that abundance all year, with only a brief pause for what passes in Napier as winter.

In the busy modern world, it is increasingly rare for children to learn about gardening from their parents, but it is the best way. Discovering early in life what it means to grow things in a garden can set patterns and habits that will last for life. It teaches young ones that flowers and all living things enrich our lives, along with other amenities like music and literature.

The slight fragrance of this nostalgic spring arrangement of clustered nosegays is perfect for a bedroom. The arrangement features auriculas, miniature striped carnations, thryptomene, Garnet roses, alstroemeria, Evangeline tulips, stock, and wax flowers.

When I first moved to New York City I lived in a second-floor apartment in a historic brownstone on Ninth Street and Second Avenue. The apartment's three windows faced south, so in the spring I installed double-layered window boxes, with one box suspended on brackets and another resting directly on the sill above. In the lower box I planted ivy, viola, and marigolds; the upper contained my herb garden of basil, chives, mint, thyme, and scented geranium. Shortly after the boxes were in bloom, a total stranger smiled at me in the corner grocery one day and said, "Hey, I saw your flowers!" Later in the week someone else on the street asked me, "Aren't you the guy with the flower boxes? They look great!" When I realized that others in the neighborhood were enjoying my gardening efforts, I began planting with an eye for the view from the sidewalk across the street, as well as from inside.

First appearances are always important and that goes for the place where you live. The front yard, the walkway to your door, even the area around the mailbox can become a setting for interesting, seasonal flowers that offer a friendly

BELOW: The dramatic form of the *Banksia praemorsa* from Western Australia demands attention, so here it is given an isolated spot in the room. When you create a "sculptural" arrangement, it should be given a little "air" so that it can be fully appreciated.

RIGHT: The earthy color scheme of this masculine room is complemented by the exuberant sunflowers arranged in an antique Spanish pitcher. The flowers are a bit of a surprise here. "Matching" flowers to rooms is a bit trite— some spontaneity should be attempted.

"hello" to welcome all who come to your door. Even delivery people and passersby will look at them fondly and imagine that someone nice lives there.

I'm delighted by window boxes in London. At any time of year they are generally planted with suitable and very agreeable combinations of hardy flowers and foliage that relieve the formal facades. The window box punctuates the bleak city landscape with welcome splashes of color and surprise. In Spain, Italy, and France, flowers dress the courtyard and doorways, becoming an inseparable part of our memory of holiday visits. Although I have seen window boxes in many cities all over the globe, to me the term *window box* will always be synonymous with Switzerland, where the vitality of the geraniums and other plants and the dedicated way the Swiss fill their windows with flowers of such brilliant color is unsurpassed in the world.

City dwellers often overlook the most obvious places outside their house or apartment where flowers could thrive. Rooftops, for example, are often empty and can provide

great space for city gardeners. The abundant sunlight up there can nourish a steady supply of flowers and vegetables and, incidentally, create a more interesting view for neighbors in the buildings around and above you. The joys of gardening—picking and smelling your own roses, indulging yourself in the feisty growth of snapdragons, savoring a fresh warm tomato—are not restricted to those with a country estate. The next time you haul your deck chair, towel, and sunbathing oils up to the roof, check out the territory. With determination, and a good-sized planter box, some soil, and a few starter plants, you are ready to begin a rooftop garden.

Of all the rooms in the home, the bedroom is where I feel we are most ourselves, where we relax, rest, restore our energy, commune with the night, and greet the new day. There we appreciate the natural fragrance and subtle colors of flowers—the soft, lulling scent of roses at night, a whiff of freesia in the morning to stir the adrenaline. The bedroom is a logical spot for flowers precisely because the arrangement need not be large or extravagant. Even a single peony or a jug of sweet peas reflected in the mirror in the glow of subtle light can make a difference.

Plants and bathrooms are made for each other when there is natural light and enough space so they don't get in the way. The warmth and humidity of the bath and shower can create the steamy, semitropical environment that suits many ferns and flowering plants, especially orchids. I particularly remember friends of mine raising cattleya and other orchid varieties in the bathroom of their wonderful old Brooklyn brownstone. They took advantage of the room's northern exposure and grew these hanging plants right in the windows, eliminating the need for shades and curtains against the curious eyes of the ever-present city neighbors. Flowering plants that belong to the gesneriad family, such as columnea and aschenanthus, will also do well in bathrooms, as will hoya in its many varieties and even the delicate, fragrant white stephanotis.

A strong piece of furniture, like this gilt mirror in an impressively decorated entry foyer, welcomes an arrangement with bravura. In an export porcelain bowl, the vibrant green viburnum, king protea, ornamental pineapple, dracaena foliage, and calathea flower spikes are regal enough.

The kitchen is often overlooked as a setting for flowers, I suppose because there is often a commotion preparing meals on time and then hurrying to clean up afterwards to get on to other activities. But what a difference flowers or plants can make, especially on the windowsill above the sink and counter in an area where we spend so much time. I've enjoyed a rabbit's foot fern (*Duvallia fejeensis*) on my windowsill for years now. I've watched it grow up from a small rooted cutting to overflow its present four-inch pot. Growing in a peat soil, it needs only about a cupful of water once a week. Nothing could be easier to keep and maintain. It has grown steadily over the years to completely surround the clay pot and bring grace and beauty to an area of the kitchen that is so often noted for its clutter. Cuttings from it have sired so many offspring I can hardly remember all the friends I have given them to. When I do give them away as gifts, especially to friends who enjoy cooking, I tell them that this little fern has grown up entirely in my kitchen, and as a "kitchen fern," it would probably do as well for them in their own kitchens.

Preparing meals or cleaning up at the kitchen counter can be much less of a chore with a view of an outdoor garden or window box in full bloom. But even two bright zinnias or a striped tulip in a simple flask sitting on a counter or windowsill can brighten this workplace and provide a sense of companionship for the solitary tasks we perform there.

I enjoy cobalt blue glass and keep a couple of short bottles and a jug on the windowsill in my kitchen breakfast room, always sporting flowers of the season. Sunlight awakens the blue accents and makes each color more appealing. Summer breakfasts and my daily lunches are always more enjoyable here because of them, along with the tall pine dresser that is loaded with fruit- and flower-decorated plates, and the view over the flowering window boxes to the woodland garden. The dappled light of summer between the trunks of giant oak trees and the autumn sun slanting through the fiery dogwood leaves highlight the changing garden. The brilliant blue of mertensia (Virginia bluebells) is a great foil for the palest pink of the Magnolia stellata. The later astilbe in a range of pink and rose provides a glowing scarf of color among the fresh greens of hosta and fern fronds. And I enjoy it all from the breakfast table.

For people on the run or a large family that needs optimum space around the table, a single flowering plant can often be the best solution for an eating area. Try a cache pot or basket with a liner to hold a cyclamen, an amaryllis plant, a bright kalanchoe, or, if the light is good enough, a hearty geranium plant.

In many households today, the dining room is used only for special occasions, especially after the kids are off to college or have left home to begin lives of their own. But this

BABY'S BREATH

Baby's breath, or gypsophila, is a florist's delight. A few sprigs of this light, graceful white or pink "filler" can transform a modest little bunch of flowers into a beguiling nosegay. And it has become an inevitable supplement to wedding bouquets and bridal veils. Because everyone seems to love it, baby's breath has become something of a cliché, but let's not dismiss it so easily.

In spite of its delicate, almost fairylike appearance, baby's breath is a hardy garden plant and occurs in annual and perennial form. The best-known variety is *Gypsophila paniculata*, an old-fashioned garden perennial native to Europe, now readily available from plant nurseries and easily grown in most parts of North America. Groups of the three-foot-high clouds of tiny white flowers make an arresting summer accent in a mixed perennial border.

Two or three long stems added to a large all-white arrangement of peony, iris, and lilac can provide contrast and an appealing, ethereal note for a wedding decoration. To my mind, however, baby's breath looks best all by itself. A silver wine cooler, for example, exploding with a soft cloud of white baby's breath might strike a surprisingly contemporary note.

Finally, gypsophila dries well right in the vase and can be recycled for winter bouquets.

PRECEDING PAGES: For a spring party, an Aztec-inspired pot provides the base for a boldly colorful arrangement of double tulips, ranunculus, lilacs, freesia, dianthus, spray roses, miniature gladioli, and delphiniums.

The arrangement includes *Vallota purpurea*, red kangaroo paw, jewels of Ophir, spider orchids "James Storeii," and flowering heads of Sedum "Vera Jameson."

BELOW: In a room where subdued pewter tones dominate, a touch of bright color serves as a terrific punctuation mark.

OPPOSITE: In a city apartment full of high-tech paraphernalia, a white phalaenopsis orchid is graphic enough to hold its own. It's also easy to grow.

setting for the traditional family meal has always been my forum for creative ideas with flowers. A dining table arrangement by definition is the ideal place to show off the latest roses from the garden along with the family silver. My guests always appreciate flowers at the dinner table, whether they are loose camellia blossoms laid right on the tablecloth or a pair of silver shells with lily of the valley carefully arranged with its own leaves. When extra guests make things a little crowded around the dining table, the sideboard can become the setting for the centerpiece. A generous sheaf of wheat tied with ribbons, set on a woven tray and surrounded with a squash, apples, and pears, makes an easily contrived but effective autumn display.

In the dining room of friends in Connecticut, I had a shallow copper tray made for the wide seat in the bay window. Covered with pale beige pea gravel, it has become a window garden of seasonal plants. My friends enjoy their mini-conservatory and find they prefer dining there rather than in the pokey kitchen, now that I have, as they say, "humanized" it. Their indoor garden is alive with dwarf orange trees, cyclamen, primula, and African violets in the winter months, and caladium, ferns, and begonia in the summer.

While the dining room may be used only occasionally, the family den or living room is probably the real center of the household, certainly when everyone is in for the weekend.

Flowers can bring a sense of calm and order to the comings and goings, the television, the music, the myriad distractions. Here I would spend a little time and effort to arrange a seasonal display: an old vine basket of hydrangea plants, with their soft, cloudlike heads of blue or rose, for a sofa table, or several handfuls of generously blooming nasturtium in a mug or two placed on the coffee table or under a side lamp. In the spring days there are so many flowers—tulips, lilacs, foxgloves, apple blossoms—that I would keep the active living quarters filled with a sample of all the garden has to offer. During the heat of the summer, settle for a tub or two of caladium under the window, a huge Boston fern for the fireplace, and a daily picking of roses and sweet peas, replaced from the garden's bounty as they fade.

The antique watering can in this spacious country kitchen is filled with dahlias, *Crocosmia lucifer*, a variety of lilies, cleome, flowering oregano, and roses (Tournament of Roses).

When I return from a long weekend or a trip, I enjoy refreshing my living spaces in the barn, filling the quiet rooms with music and movement, cooking up something in the kitchen, and letting the smells drift through the house—and more importantly, putting flowers in my favorite vases and bringing the plants in from the yard or conservatory. Then I know I'm home. The flowers do it for me every time. It's a tired cliché, but like most clichés it speaks a time-honored truth: flowers bring a room to life. They animate our surroundings and our spirits. Although I try not to, I subconsciously gauge the lives of the people I meet and the life in their homes by whether or not I find fresh flowers in the rooms where they spend most of the time. Flowers do give a room a touch of your own personality and speak of what is meaningful to you, no matter if the signal is quiet and modest or loud and clear.

Flowers in the Workplace

Flowers often reveal the warm, gentle qualities of the people who grow them; and I find gentle, appreciative attitudes in my friends who care about gardens and flowers. Flowers always make a positive statement about our appreciation of things. This is why we bring flowers into the workroom, the study, or the office—any place where we spend time over activities that we do for a living or the hobbies that make life more enjoyable. An old copper kettle filled with bright zinnias, or a magnolia branch in the spring with just a couple of blossoms bursting from it really wakes up a home, office, or studio. It can be a pleasant surprise to find flowers where we least expect them, thriving under a grow lamp in a basement workroom, for example, where the lack of light would lead us to assume flowers would be out of the question. Plant lights can transform a basement apartment or an interior office space, and allow a whole range of foliage and flowering plants to thrive.

For flower lovers who work in drab city offices, a pot of early spring tulips placed on a gray filing cabinet will illuminate the cold, impersonal decor and announce to coworkers and clients alike that warm personable people work there. The unexpected flower in a place of routine can change everything. Try it for yourself. When you pack your running shoes, tennis racket, sack lunch, and head for work on a Monday morning, stop to pick up a few flowers for your desk as well.

Flowers have a great way of breaking down social barriers between people, and we find out that we really do have things in common with one another. Whether it's the C.E.O., an elevator operator, a new client, or a reception clerk, all appreciate the impact flowers make in an office. Have you ever noticed that the receptionist with flowers on her desk, who sounded so gruff over the phone, is really a warm and friendly human being after all? Acknowledging our love of flowers is a way of acknowledging our common humanity. Try flowers in the board room as a calming element before an important meeting. They may be the perfect icebreaker.

Flowers in Public Places

Living with flowers involves our enjoyment of them beyond our private homes and work spaces. Encountering flowers in the great public places of the city can be equally rewarding, especially for urban captives who seldom get out to the country or see a suburban garden. New Yorkers walk out of their way at Rockefeller Center to see what new surprises are offered in the changing installations at the famous Channel Gardens.

This small oasis leading to the summer café and winter skating rink is a magnet for tourists, particularly the flower-minded, for good reason. Over the years the outstanding quality of the plant material and the exceptional

In early spring it may be too chilly to have lunch outdoors, so why not bring the garden inside? Arranged in a naturalistic grouping on a shallow Peking glass plate are Narcissus "Tête-à-tête," winter aconite, snowdrops, *Cyclamen coum*, specie crocus, and *Iris reticulata*, set in a bed of green moss.

creativity behind the changing display have gained it the distinction of being a unique horticultural theater and have stimulated city planners around the world. Fortunately, New Yorkers' passion for flowers has also been addressed by the Park Avenue Gardens, the newly restored Central Park Conservatory Garden, and the new green of Battery Park City, as well as the countless open malls and parks with seating and plantings that have become part of city life over the past twenty or so years.

In the early 1970s I was asked to take over the seasonal plantings and garden maintenance of Greenacre Park on East 51st Street, one of New York's first "vest-pocket parks" that shelters a hospitable environment of plants, flowers, and waterfalls in the heart of midtown Manhattan. Here residents of neighboring hotels and apartment buildings sit and talk to friends; the park is their living room. Office workers crowd in for lunch outdoors. Throughout the day the tiny microcosm teems with life—students paging through textbooks before class, young mothers walking their babies in strollers, harried shoppers resting their feet. The peace and tranquility is truly amazing; the place exudes balance and well-being by injecting greenery and colorful flowers into the tight vertical landscape of the city. The roaring sound of the great cascade waterfall provides the "white noise" that drowns out the traffic noise and the jarring screams of sirens.

I enjoy watching tourists or visitors stumble into Greenacre Park and I like to catch their response and surprise. Imagine (their faces say), finally a pretty place to sit, enjoy a cup of coffee, and see a calmer side of New York City. The container plantings change seasonally with heather, hyacinths, and pansies in March; forsythia, cineraria, and tulips in April; bromeliads, ferns, and palms throughout the tropical summer, until the crisp days of fall bring the golden shimmer of locust leaves that lie over the red and rusty mum plants. Brightly berried hollies and ever-

The bathroom is a place where flowers are unexpected. This child's bathroom is brightened up with an appropriately "naive" nosegay of balloon flowers, "love-in-a-mist," dwarf sunflowers, red salvia, cat mint, and cosmos.

greens take the park through the winter months—and we're back in spring. It's almost like being a guest in a private garden, a rather unique experience in New York City.

Philanthropy at its best is providing funding for flowers in public places, such as the much-admired gift of Lila Acheson Wallace that has kept glorious, colorful bouquets of fresh flowers in the great foyer of the Metropolitan Museum since the 1970s. These always spectacular urns of seasonal flowers are enjoyed by the thousands of daily visitors throughout the year and have been an incentive for similar projects in other museums around the country. "Thank you, Mrs. Wallace," I say every time I enter the museum, "for sharing your love and appreciation for flowers in such a generous way." Even though the setting is grand and formal, the gift becomes completely personal when we walk through the front door and we get the feeling that those magnificent displays were arranged for each of us personally.

I wish that city councils and the philanthropic interests of every city would join forces to plant and care for flowers wherever possible: around parking lots, traffic circles, downtown sidewalks, median strips on highways, and at toll booths. Intelligent landscaping and urban design can incorporate flowers into many areas of town and city life and instill a sense of pride in citizens that can never be matched in dollars and cents.

It's especially reassuring when public-spirited citizens involve themselves at whatever level in funding or arranging for flower displays for public events or community services. Those who do find great satisfaction in sharing their love of flowers and making others smile. For example, through the generosity of Enid Haupt, a great flower lover and gardener noted for her funding of the rebuilt greenhouse at the New York Botanic Gardens, a display and working greenhouse attached to the Howard Rusk Institute at New York University Hospital provides a practical hands-on opportunity for patients to get their hands dirty and their spirits uplifted by caring for flowers and plants throughout the year.

Flowers are an important part of public life. Their ritual use at civic and social affairs is deeply rooted in human history. From the Greek theaters and Roman circuses to opening nights at Covent Garden and premieres at the Met, lavish flowers frame the spectacle and honor the artists when the performance ends. It is one of our finest traditions. Even if it is limited to an Easter display of lilies in the cathedral or the man-made trees of poinsettia plants in the shopping mall at Christmas, a chance to enjoy the beauty of flowers in public places enriches urban life.

Anytime I'm at the Plaza Hotel in New York City I love to watch tourists walk in for their first glimpse of that great lobby and the Palm Court. Enchanted by the orchestral trio, the potted palms, the chandeliers, and a sense of history, their eyes turn immediately to the flowers. And often the weary tourist, a little glazed by the oppressive man-made environment of the city, will exclaim on seeing the flowers close up, "Oh, they're real!" Since so much in today's world is not real, fresh flowers can come as a surprise. They are not frozen in concrete, molded in plastic, or made out of cardboard. They are gloriously, transiently real—the constant, natural participants in the theater of the changing seasons.

Speaking of places that are not real, urban malls have come under extensive criticism for creating plastic worlds of glitter dedicated to crass materialism. But whatever personal feelings we have about them—either as a boon to easy shopping or a bane on the suburban landscape—the more enlightened developers have reserved places for flowers. Skylights, fountains, and walk-through gardens of carefully scaled displays of trees and flowering plants can make the

A library table is transformed from a workplace when guests are expected. This end-of-summer arrangement uses garden-variety flowers to make a grand statement.

Arranged are butterfly delphinium, *Phlox peniculata* "Blue Ice," seed heads of *Filapendula rubra, Hydrangea arborescens*, and Artemesia "Silver King."

modern mall a pleasant and welcoming environment, one that changes with the seasons naturally, in spite of its hermetically sealed climate.

For the last several years, I have provided the Christmas decorations for Manhattan's South Street Seaport, a mini-shopping city located in a historically preserved area of nineteenth-century wharfs and warehouses. In the past we have tried to create a display in keeping with the setting, with living trees in tubs and barrels and roping made from a variety of fresh-cut greenery. We added different trims with a nineteenth-century flavor, as if the merchants themselves had a say in the colors and details: gingham, plaid, wooden toys, glazed fruit—all reflect the mood and feel of the nineteenth-century market. When thoughtfully designed, even the slickest mall can become a pleasant refuge from the monotonous asphalt of parking lots and interstate highways, by providing spaces for gardens and floral settings to capture the living spirit of each season.

SPECIAL OCCASIONS

RIGHT: To dress up unsightly tent poles for an autumn party, buckets strapped to the tops of the poles serve as the containers for bittersweet and crab apple branches, goldenrod, gladioli, and chrysanthemums.

PRECEDING PAGES: The deep laquer-red walls of this dining room provide a great foil for a variety of colors. Here spicy colored dwarf-callas, ranunculus, orange *Ornithalgum dubia*, and hypericum berries warm up a winter night.

FOLLOWING PAGES: A spring party deserves an appropriate color scheme. Pinks, roses, and lavenders have been chosen for this event. Tubs of hydrangeas with variegated ivy and plants of such perennials as dahlia, foxglove, and astilbe in pots convey the "feeling" of May.

THE LATE PHOTOGRAPHER Horst, who was my neighbor and good friend, was in Germany one summer for a week of photographing when he was suddenly taken ill and rushed to the hospital. What was intended to be a week of work turned into a month of treatment. When he recovered enough to be released, he decided that the best therapy was to come home to Long Island. Although I could not meet him at the airport, I decided to welcome him home in my own way—with flowers.

I combed my gardens and the market for the brightest and best flowers that were in full bloom and literally filled his home with them. The front door, the living room, dining room, bedroom, and even the bath were bright with summer color: scabious, lilies and cosmos, Joe Pye weed, plus lots of white caladiums with pink and white lily plants in large baskets. Clusters of pink lily heads and full roses placed in silver tankards ran the length of the dining-room table. The house radiated optimism, cheerfulness, and good health. And the message was clear: I was there in spirit even though I had to be miles away that day.

In my experience, there is no substitute for flowers to enhance the atmosphere on all the important occasions of family life when the house needs a little extra "dressing up":

a sweet sixteen party, a graduation celebration, a wedding anniversary, a family christening. Although arranging flowers may mean a little extra work, they will most certainly earn extra applause; and guests and friends will appreciate your efforts and your style.

Family Celebrations

The theme of the occasion can direct our choices and decisions but should not ride roughshod over our personal preferences or the favorite flower of an honored guest. A spring christening, for example, suggests to me the pale colors of the sweet peas, early roses, lilies of the valley, sprays of daphne, and sweetly scented *Viburnum carlesii*. Christenings are perfect for small gathered nosegays, arranged right in your hand, tied with a ribbon, and then set in silver christening mugs or similar low bowls, which could be placed down the length of the dining table. These small fragrant flowers in pale colors perfectly complement an occasion centered on the newborn baby.

Somehow a sweet sixteen party at home brings to mind wreaths of pink sweetheart roses around candlesticks with ribbon, bouquets of sweet peas, and baby's breath on frothy tablecloths of lace or white Swiss muslin. But the season of the year will dictate what the garden has to offer. In winter, yellow flowering jasmine and miniature daffodils in a planted dish garden, arranged in a naturalistic way in moss, might be appropriate. Simple pink camellia blossoms spread as a garland with ribbons at the center of each table might be "just adorable" enough to be perfect.

Friends attending a family graduation party may not always notice the details of the special table centerpiece, even if you've chosen the graduate's favorite flowers. They will, however, certainly respond to a family setting itself made more attractive, more composed, serene, and frankly beautiful by fresh flowers that say, "Hello, do come in and

join us; we're having a party." In their unique way, even a few flowers in the spaces you live in make each hour of the day something of a special occasion.

Within the family, sentimental association can link certain flowers with birthdays and anniversaries, and it's fun to try to find those appropriate to the occasion. "Don't you remember grandma carried those calla lilies at her wedding, and Aunt May received lilies of the valley when David was born?" When we decide to celebrate at home rather than at a restaurant, hotel, or club, we make the initial decision that this party is going to be personal. The flowers I choose become part of the day and visibly spread their color and form throughout the house. They are also guests at the party, to be admired and enjoyed. Perhaps it's fall: gather branches of bright Japanese maple leaves with amber-yellow lilies on

PRECEDING PAGE: Tiered topiaries of boxwood and ivy decorated with grapevine, lilies, and roses create a dramatic interior landscape.

ABOVE: Celebrate the summer with roses. A rather opulent Mediterranean atmosphere is created here with toile table cloths and bouquets of garden roses, such as French Lace, Just Joey, Brandy, and Shreveport, combined with hydrangea, eucalyptus, and sword fern in shallow terracotta bowls.

the hall table and use rosebuds, crab apples, and wild rose hips to decorate the candlecups for the buffet, with a few full rose petals strewn on the cloth below, and everything will look wonderful. The candlelight, the tablecloth, the good friends, and table settings—everything looks and feels better in a setting enhanced by the natural beauty of flowers.

In the course of my work I'm asked to provide flowers for many formal occasions, but the vast majority are wedding parties. Booking a florist is as much a priority today as arranging for a photographer, reserving a banquet room, and notifying the church. Some wedding parties on my schedule are booked as much as a year in advance, which shows how important flowers are for the occasion. I'm sure flowers will always be part of weddings. Not even the rebelliousness of the 1960s, which discarded so much of what was old and traditional, managed to eliminate flowers from the wedding scene. While young couples may have forsaken the church and traditional bridal clothing, they moved the wedding outdoors into the garden or meadow, where flowers were even more abundant. The youthful exuberance that sought a return to nature and to doing things in more informal ways led to marriage ceremonies performed even closer to where flowers grow, in the out-of-doors.

In decorating the church, I place the flowers strategically where they will be admired without being obtrusive: tubs of flowering plants in the porch or foyer, on pedestals to flank the altar table, nosegays on the pews to decorate the aisle, and even in swags over doorways. If the wedding is at home, the bridal party might choose to stand beneath a floral archway as a substitute for the gothic arches of the church. Here flowers will change the home into an appropriate place for the wedding ceremony. The familiar archway separating the living room and dining room takes on a special beauty, even grandeur, when decorated with a garland of greenery and flowers caught with ribbons. During a Jewish wedding, the couple stands under a specially significant

ABOVE: For a summer wedding luncheon, the seahorse urn is filled with trails of wild knotweed, ivy, *Amaranthus viridus*, and hosta leaves. Flowers are heads of Sedum "Autumn Joy," and Fresca lilies. Rose and sedum centerpieces continue the color scheme.

FOLLOWING PAGE: The romantic fragrance of peonies, roses, jasmine, and campanula with variegated ivy to set them off is chosen for a June wedding reception. The shaded candlesticks will illuminate the party into the evening hours.

canopy called a Chuppah, which is often a bower decorated entirely with flowers. Flowers spring up everywhere on wedding days: the bouquets for the bride and her attendants, the groomsmen's boutonnieres, the rosebuds and ribbons woven in circlets for the flower girl's hair, even on the wedding cake, squeezed out in icing with meticulous care. And when the couple leaves the church, we shower them with petals. How could there be a wedding without flowers?

Springtime always turns our thoughts to its special flowers, love, and new life. Easter wouldn't be quite the same without flowers. Whether celebrated in a sacred or secular manner, the Easter season is the time for green grass, fresh young leaves, and the excitement of new buds opening in the garden. With Easter come hyacinths, lilies, azaleas, primroses, and daffodils—all to highlight the world turning green and colorful again.

One year in the early spring I was in Greece exploring historic sites. It had been a harsh, cold winter throughout Europe that year, and it was a welcome miracle to discover

almond blossoms, tiny wild anemones, primroses, and specie irises blooming once again up in the mountains. On my travels I am always amazed to see how flowers grow spontaneously and in generous variety around many sacred places. I like to think there is some universal and continuous connection between flowers and the ruins of the cities of ancient Greece. Around these sites, even where centuries of tourists have altered the approaches and immediate environs, nature sees to it that she has the final say by sending up the very flowers that have grown there since those ancient times. At Olympia, anemones, scillas, and irises fill the stadium and line the athletes' way every spring. With flowers, nature renders the spot still a meeting place for both humans and deities.

One evening in the course of this trip, my three companions and I decided to see Delphi by moonlight. That night we began the ascent to Delphi dressed warmly because the air was damp and chilly. The sky was clear and a crisp full moon lit our way as we walked the ancient stones of the approach to the temple. As we passed through a tunnel of olive trees, a dark figure stepped from the shadows and murmured a respectful "Kalysperos" and to my great surprise handed each of us a branch of white almond blossom, a luminous magic staff in the moonlight. The mysterious stranger turned out to be a guide who had suspected someone would be coming to enjoy the splendors of Delphi beneath a full moon, and he was happy to be on hand to officiate, as well as to earn his tip. Magic can happen easily and in simple unexpected ways in sacred places, and the memory of that evening remains indelible for many reasons, not the least of which was the almond blossoms given to us.

Flowers bring their touch of magic to any joyful occasion, and since so many of these center around a family dinner, I believe we should make full use of them at the dining table. Whether the occasion is formal or informal, the table offers a unique forum for floral decorations. Flowers attract the attention and provide friendly, unobtrusive insights into

PRECEDING PAGE: Roses gathered from the garden and simply arranged are the perfect accent for a summer luncheon.

ABOVE: The tall pedestal arrangements here were created for a grand Russian-themed ball in late summer. Flowers used include tropical ginger, knotweed chrysanthemums, lilies, amaranthus, sea lavender, and hydrangea.

OPPOSITE: The combination of the classic rose "Message" and the "Cleopatra" with trails of *Jasmin polyanthum*, "Glacier" ivy, hypericum berries, and accents of green euphorbia are just one possibility to dress this thirty-three-inch-high candelabra for a party.

FOLLOWING PAGES, LEFT: For a midsummer dinner in New York's Central Park, the flowers are raised above the table on a coiled spring of my own design. White, pale pink, and green flowers were chosen to produce a "cool" look. Black tablecloths and chairs help to minimize the volume of the furniture. White peonies and larkspur, La Rêve lilies, and asters make up the soothing arrangements.

FOLLOWING PAGES, RIGHT: Homage to Sheila Macqueen: When the distinguished English flower arranger came for afternoon tea, I fashioned this whimsy for the tea table, with white callicarpa, snowberry, buddleia, meidiland roses, and hydrangea to frame mixed garden roses and the striped rose "soutine."

These lion topiaries, holding baskets of spring tulips, lilies, delphiniums, quince, and asters, were made by Barbara Gallop. One could make a smaller version for home use with a wire frame covered with chicken wire and sheet moss.

what is unique and personal about the host or hostess. Each table setting gives us a chance to indulge our private tastes, be creative, express ourselves in a medium everyone can appreciate and enjoy. It allows us to show off in the best sense of that term, combining our favorite flowers with foliage, fruits, and berries, with the silver, china ware, tablecloths, and candles.

Brunches, even though they are planned, seem spontaneous, and flowers should reflect this. The relaxed, worry-free atmosphere of Saturday or Sunday brunch should set the tone for the flowers and table setting in general. It's daytime, so forget the candles. Use flowers you find at the farm stand, or pick a roadside bouquet of grasses, Queen Anne's lace, and black-eyed Susans still damp with the morning dew. It's fun finding them, looking for that naive touch of beauty in the weeds and wildlands. Choose some red poppies, columbines, or zinnias and crowd them into a pottery mug, or cut them short and arrange them in a low casserole (chicken wire crumpled in the container is the trick here).

If you are near the seaside, celebrate the morning with bright primary colors that reflect the maritime tones of golden sun, blue sea, and multicolored pennants flapping against white sails. For example, tuck yellow and red hibiscus blossoms into the cavities of a large lump of white coral, fill skinny French bread baskets with hedges of blue cornflowers and bright green parsley, or stuff red geranium nosegays into blue glass tumblers. Keep the morning arrangements fresh and unstudied, as friendly as a simple greeting that says, "Glad you stopped by."

Because I live with flowers, I don't have to go to great lengths to bring them in on special occasions. I just move them around. A pot of geraniums in full roar on the patio can come onto the porch or into the den for the monthly bridge party. Some red petunias, fuchsias, or roses can combine with a basket of bright apples for the tea table. For a centerpiece, dress up a topiary herb such as a standard rosemary, scented geranium, or myrtle from the summer yard just by adding a party bow and don't worry about what your friends will say. They've come to see *you* and they'll enjoy your creative efforts. I don't think you even need a formal arrangement if you want your friends to feel comfortable in your home. For the bridge crowd, you might simply put together three small baskets of cherry tomatoes and nasturtiums as a centerpiece and give one to each of your guests at the end of the party as a take-home gift. This thoughtfulness says more about you than a fancy arrangement from the florist.

Harvest Time

I remember one Thanksgiving in New Zealand when my family had befriended an American military man stationed there with Operation Deepfreeze, the United States' mission to the South Pole. We planned to give him as traditional a Thanksgiving feast as we could, especially when we learned that he would supply the turkey. Obviously we were not going to find pumpkins and bittersweet vine in New

Zealand in November. That's springtime down under. Still I knew that Americans' emotional ties to Thanksgiving are largely distilled from the colors, images, and fragrances of autumn. It is a little difficult to fake that unique combination of seasonal ingredients that make up the magic of the harvest season: orange pumpkins, turkey roasting in the oven, the smell of wood smoke on the chill air, the mulchy scent of fallen leaves piled on the damp ground. National holidays become very personal celebrations, filled with memory and emotion. So for our "orphaned" American I suggested the harvest by simply arranging two fat sheaves of dried wheat on the dining table anchored around the candlesticks with bows of amber velvet ribbon. He was delighted and appreciated our efforts, even though we couldn't duplicate all the trimmings of a traditional American Thanksgiving dinner. Our Maori kumara as stand-in for sweet potatoes, our version of pecan pie, and the smell of the roasting turkey were just enough touches to arouse the fond memories of his home and family.

The shapes and smells of harvest time can be brought indoors as early as Halloween and kept or freshened up through Thanksgiving. Pumpkins, squash, sheaves of wheat or oats, wild grapevine, Indian corn, as well as the traditional autumn flowers: wreaths of bittersweet vine, late asters, crab apples, mums. Use your imagination to make the familiar different, and don't be cowardly. Find settings for them that you haven't used before: the empty fireplace, the top of a chest or cupboard, the stair bannister, the upstairs landing. In Sweden, I remember the generous sheaves of oats set out in winter for the birds tied to the tops of long poles with bright ribbons or tucked up under the eaves out of the reach of field mice. Dress up the house for fall with a basket of bright leaves, late roses, and especially the drying wildflowers that catch our breath with their brilliant color as they live out their last days so dramatically against the fading greens of summer.

GODS, HEROES, AND FLOWERS

To the ancient Greeks, flowers were often part of a cycle of metamorphosis in which nature and human life seemed forever intertwined. In countless myths, men, women, and plants share a common flow of energy, sometimes appearing in human shape, sometimes in floral. Flowers rise from the shed tears of lovers and mourners and appear at the birth of gods. Iris was goddess of the Rainbow, and in Greek mythology acted as messenger from the gods, a link between Olympus and mortals since she touched both sky and earth. The asphodel springs from the blood of heroes. Hyacinth represents the ideal beauty of youth. Venus's slipper is commemorated by an orchid. The handsome Narcissus bequeathed his name to a flower that now belongs only to him. Daphne not only gave her name to a bay tree, but she actually turned into one. The Madonna lily (*Lilium candidum*) has been associated with human activity since the earliest days of antiquity, the oldest illustration being the wall painting at Amnisos, near Knossos in Crete, made about 1550 B.C.

PRECEDING PAGES: An afternoon tea is made special with roses, including Royal Highness, Levand, and Color Magic, with buddleia, "love-in-a-mist" seed pods, and eucalyptus buds.

BELOW: When getting married at home, one can create a special setting. Here, an arch of twigs and vines links two raised arrangements and columns swathed in ivy.

OPPOSITE: For a party in late summer, an abundant arrangement of whatever is blooming in the garden serves as a welcome mat to guests. For this entry hall a restrained color scheme was chosen, using dahlias, Japanese anemones, Queen Anne's lace, lilies, and eucalyptus foliage.

Winter Holidays

If any holiday says "home," it is Christmas. The Yuletide calls everyone home, if only in spirit, to return and spend time in a family setting as we pass through the shortest days of the year and longest, darkest nights. When I moved up to the northern hemisphere, I came to appreciate a winter Christmas as the proper kind: snow, bare trees, and the house coming alive with people home for the winter holidays. As in olden times, when the Norse gods were beseeched for protection against the harsh elements and druids looking for the maverick sprig of mistletoe growing on the sacred oak appeased the winter deities with offerings, gift-giving has been part of the Yuletide season. Gifts and special remembrances are an exciting part of these holidays in my world, and flowers, of course, play their part as companions to the gaily wrapped packages under the tree. Flowering bulbs, amaryllis, narcissus, or hyacinth make welcome gifts, as do seeds and plants of fragrant herbs, a lemon tree, or a young bay tree.

Bringing evergreens indoors during the winter solstice is an ancient custom in northern Europe. Holly, ivy, spruce, and pine remind us that spring will come just as surely as these boughs keep their fresh green color through the coldest months. In them, as in the Christmas tree itself, we recognize the promise of rebirth that is spring. The lights and candles of Christmas shining brightly in the twilight of shortened days joyfully announce that the sun and spring will soon return.

For an outdoor wedding, an aisle of columns with flowered capitals makes for a spectacular setting. A flower-decorated arbor in front provides a place to exchange vows.

I found it an extraordinary sight in Sweden on the winter feast of Saint Lucia to see young girls in white robes walk through the snowy streets wearing delicate wreaths with tiny candles on their heads. In celebrating the Festival of Light they too were witnesses to the belief that even what is gentle and tender contains human strength and courage capable of surviving the wintry months.

With its pure white flowers, the *Helleborus niger*, or winter rose, is as distinctively Christmas for the English as the poinsettia is for Americans. Combined with holly and pine, it makes a beautiful winter bouquet, quite unlike the flowers seen in homes in the United States. All seasonal holidays grow out of a region's natural climate and environment, along with the region's natural flora and fauna. Not every part of the United States is under the cold, clammy hand of winter that slaps us around on the northeast coast. In Seattle, for example, the winter cherry (*Prunus subhirtella "Autumnalis"*) blooms at Christmas even with ice crystals on the blossoms. In New Zealand, Christmas means lilies, especially *Lilium regale*, the famous native of China. Since it blooms naturally in midsummer, around December 25, it has become the traditional Christmas flower for Kiwis. A whiff of the unique fragrance can transport me right back to Christchurch, my flower shop there, and those holiday deliveries.

For more than twenty years I had the responsibility of providing flowers and aisle decorations for the prestigious Winter Antiques Show at Manhattan's Seventh Regiment Armory on Park Avenue. It opens just one month after

HOW TO USE A CANDLECUP

The candlecup is the solution for making the most of a very few flowers when there's not much room on the table. With a candlecup we can create elegant flower arrangements on candlesticks of any style—from a low china or wooden candlestick to an elegant five-arm silver candelabra—and make use of short-stemmed flowers that might be otherwise difficult to arrange. Pansies, roses, honeysuckle, primulas, jasmine, azaleas, and sweet peas are some of my favorites.

Oasis is the key. Cut a square of dry oasis to fit the round cup, and mound it like a well-stuffed ice cream cone. Secure the mound with two narrow strips of floral tape across the sides. Submerge the candlecup in water until the bubbles cease. Place the candlecup in the candlestick, and if needed, secure it with a little floral or modeling clay.

Push the candle into place and then arrange the flowers, usually trailing material to hang down and reach out, with the low, full flowers crowning the top. Obviously the flowers should not be set high up close to the flame but around the top of the cup. With long tables I prefer 18-inch tapers, which will burn longer and keep the flame above eye level. On a five-branch candelabra I recommend just one central arrangement with four candles.

Flowers can last in a candlecup for an amazing length of time. You will find that by replacing the old candle an arrangement can be used again. Just lift the candlecup from the candlestick, enclose it in a plastic bag, and store it in a cool, dark place, such as the bottom of the refrigerator. If the oasis is kept moist and cool, you can enjoy your decoration for several days.

Christmas and would get my working year and the social season off to a flying start. The decorations would often use enormous branches of Chinese quince and forsythia, which is not naturally in bloom in New York until April. I would begin cutting and forcing the branches right around Christmas and in four weeks they would be ready to burst into their golden extravagance as the show opened. I certainly enjoy "making spring happen early" during the stream of holiday parties and celebrations that, while repeating the winter themes, lead inevitably to spring. A major part of my New Year enjoyment is to hear the delight in the voices that ask me, "Wherever did you find those lilacs, tulips, and anemones at this time of year?"

BELOW: A green tree, lights, and an abundance of poinsettias are the essence of Christmas. One needn't have a tree; a wreath or some greens will create the appropriate holiday spirit. Keep decorations simple, however. Ribbons, bows, and beads are as satisfying as expensive ornaments.

OPPOSITE: Flowers can be a conversation piece. This cocktail-party setting is graced by an arrangement of striking waratah, an Australian wildflower available only in September, the beginning of spring "down under." Cattelya orchids are a companion to these flowers that lend a sophisticated seasonal touch to an event.

Outdoor Gatherings

As warmer weather begins to arrive, our thoughts turn naturally to spending time outdoors. Picnics, cookouts, evening meals on the patio become almost obsessions, so eager are we to get back outside in the fresh air and shake off the doldrums of winter claustrophobia. Again, the table becomes the center of attraction. Flowers ought to call to mind rustic, outdoor, vigorous qualities if they are to fit into the outdoor scheme.

As the summer season arrives, all those fabulous summer outings start to appear on our calendars: music festivals, concerts in the park, outdoor arts-and-crafts shows. I always look forward to those occasions when we can take a picnic, spread a tablecloth on the grass, and enjoy ourselves for a moment away from the crowds. Champagne, cold chicken, shrimp, fruit, cheese, and bread make an elegant, easy outdoor meal. And to give it that little something "extra," I include flowers. Packed in with the ice and champagne, they stay cool and fresh even in the hottest weather. As we say in New York, "Too much is never enough."

Use what seems right and appropriate for the out-of-doors rather than a vase of flowers from the house. Low tubs crammed with scented geranium or clay pots with miniature rose plants that usually stand along the edge of the patio could be wiped clean and placed on the picnic table, either in the center or down at one end. Flowers from the cutting garden or from along the driveway can be picked just before the occasion and arranged on the table, their stems inserted into a watermelon. Simply remove one large slice and make the melon your vase for a gathering of short-stemmed flowers, such as phlox, in mixed colors, with roses, bright blue salvia, or lemon and white zinnias. An evening meal needs light, so let a hurricane lamp serve as a centerpiece by encircling it with a simple wreath of summer wildflowers, hibiscus blooms, or full roses, either laid au naturel or with their stems kept fresh in an oasis ring.

Decorating the table for special occasions with flowers is a home tradition that can be carried over to the office or workplace. Office parties to celebrate holidays or birthdays need all the help they can get to alter the mood from work

LEFT: A dinner party can be a celebration. Roses are the theme here. They decorate the china, linens, and wine glasses. The centerpiece consists of miniature rose plants set with ivy in a basket. Scattered on the table are tiny nosegays of viola.

BELOW: Standing blackamoor pedestals hold a refined collection of spring flowers for a Venetian masked ball: tulips, roses, anemonies, orchids, tuberose, and freesia.

to play. The warm, special touch of flowers brings a civilizing influence that is often missing in sleek, sterile office decor. Imagine a generous basket of multicolored snapdragons in the board room on the eighty-sixth floor of the World Trade Center! Flowers calm us, slow us down, remind us that real, live human beings inhabit these places of work and routine. Even a modest arrangement to your specifications picked up at the nearby florist on a coffee break can convey your touch and express your own personality and hopes for the occasion. The flowers announce that the luncheon or party is meant to be enjoyable, even while work has to go on during that time. Flowers can even grace the driest occasions, such as presentations to clients or business luncheons. Those of us who live with flowers at home are usually willing to make the effort to enjoy them as part of our professional lives as well.

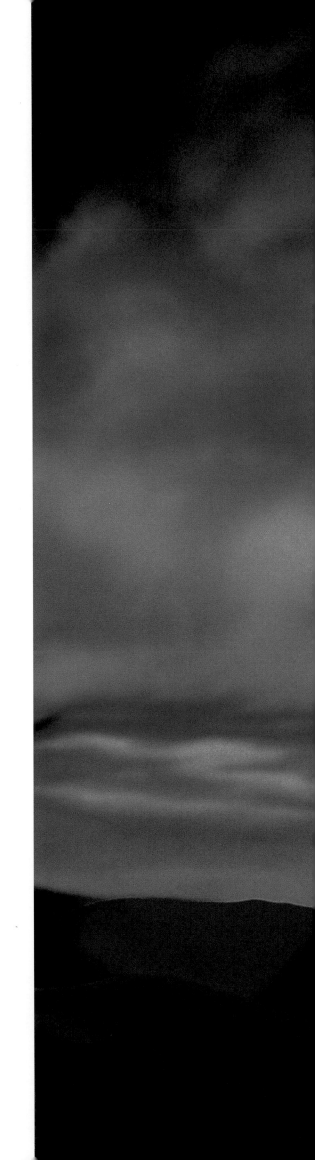

FLOWERS
AS
GIFTS

N SPITE OF THE SHOP-WORN CLICHÉ
that flowers speak louder than words, I still think flowers make the perfect gift on more occasions than one
might suspect. Beyond the traditional tokens for Mother's
Day or Valentine's Day—often the woeful offerings of your
"friendly international flower service"—a gift of flowers
can delight your friends, especially if you gather and arrange
them yourself. Because flowers can say so many things, they
fit just about every occasion: an anniversary or birthday, a
hospital visit, a mother with her new baby, or just simply to
say "thank you" or "I'm sorry." Flowers are absolutely non-
threatening—they don't require permanent storage, and
their transience is part of their charm.

Surely it is the thought that always counts, and size and
expense are not the criteria. For my friends who enjoy their
gardens, I have little trouble coming up with original gifts.
In early spring, I can lift a clump of favorite primroses or
auriculas with a trowel—soil, roots, and all—and set them
in a low clay pan or a small plastic-lined basket, finish off
with a collar of green moss and a ribbon, and I'm off to
dinner. Even that convenient bottle of wine can be doubly
welcome if it comes with a cluster of climbing roses tied to
the neck of the bottle with a festive bow. Too sensitive? Then
let the wine bottle rest in a basket among those suddenly
abundant tomatoes, with a side order of roses.

When I lived on the Norwegian island of Malmoya
while working to found an English-language theater company, I stayed in a romantic villa on the grounds where there
had once been a monastery. Seeds from plants the monks
had cultivated came up every year, flourishing in spite of the
severe Scandinavian climate. Whenever I was invited out to
dinner or visited friends, I could arrange a posy of wildflowers or create a tiny dish garden with plants from among
the rocks or in the woods. I had my pick of wild oregano
with its soft lavender rose flowers and fragrance, the cerise
blooms of wild cranesbill with brightly colored fall foliage,

ABOVE: For an early summer welcome home, graduation, or anniversary present, garden peonies, lilacs, apple blossom, azaleas, lilies, rhododendrons, and fuchsias—nature's bounty— are a perfect combination.

OPPOSITE: Potted herbs and topiaries make great gifts and are long-lasting. The boxwood topiary here is studded with roses, allium flowers, and brodiaea.

FOLLOWING PAGES: If buying a vase, shaving mug, or champagne bucket as a gift, fill it with flowers for an extra touch. This Mexican silver nautilus-shell vase is dressed up with blue hydrangea, French Lace roses, and blue "love-in-a-mist."

PRECEDING PAGE: *Photograph by Horst.*

POTPOURRI

The early Egyptians were possibly the first to experiment with potpourri (a French term that literally means "rotten pot"). They sealed vast quantities of roses in jars for use in later ceremonies. This is the traditional "moist" method of combining fragrant flowers, such as jasmine, lavender, and orange blossom, with herbs, roots, spices, and oils, then placing them in jars that are stored for a season until the various fragrances enhance each another. Today we pour the mixture into open jars and bowls to scent various rooms in the house.

The simpler "dry" method uses similar materials. Gather fragrant flowers such as lavender, roses, pansies, and broom. For color, add marigolds, delphiniums, and cornflowers. Pick on a fine day at peak bloom, or save the petals from cut flowers. Spread the petals to dry on a rack, such as an old window screen, place them in single layers on foil in trays, and dry them quickly in a low oven with the door open. Combine in a large bowl with a fixative, such as orris root or gum benzoin, along with dried herbs, slices of citrus peel, or cloves. Add drops of lavender, lemon, cinnamon, sandalwood, rose geranium, or peppermint oil to extend the fragrance.

There are many different recipes for creating a batch of potpourri. Here is one of my favorites: combine one quart of dried rose petals with one heaping tablespoon each of crushed nutmeg, cinnamon, allspice, mace, and cloves. Add a heaping tablespoon of dried and ground orange peel, three drops of eucalyptus oil, five drops of peppermint oil, and one tablespoon of lavender flowers. Blend gently and pile up in your prettiest bowl or store in a covered jar.

the early blue hepatica, or wild anemone (which is always a special treasure for me), along with varieties of buttercup, ladies bedstraw, valerian, cowslip, cornflower, harebell, and later in the summer, blueberries and wild strawberries. These wildings looked perfect with very little arrangement, and in my own house they offered overseas guests another unexpected aspect of Scandinavia.

The next time you're inclined to buy flowers for a gift because there's nothing in the garden, look outside again. Even in winter there may be some wonderful leftovers from late summer and autumn: dried grasses, seed heads, berries, a bird's nest, all just waiting to be rescued and brought indoors or worked into a gift along with a few bought flowers.

BELOW: A modest gift of a charming Victorian vase includes freesia, rosebuds, hyacinths, pink pieris, and viola.

OPPOSITE: An extravagant gift of flowers—for a welcome-home greeting, the birthday of a gardener, or to grace the front lawn of a new home—consists of an old wheelbarrow carrying an exuberant arrangement of single and double hollyhocks, giant cow parsley, ostrich feather astilbe, hydrangea, giant Scotch thistle, honeysuckle, delphiniums, phlox, specie lilies, and giant allium. (*Photograph by Horst.*)

Naturally, flowers are an appropriate gift for "flower nuts," avid gardeners, and fellow horticulturists. It is not a case of "bringing coals to Newcastle" to arrive on the doorstep with flowers, bulbs, or seeds. Gardeners love to receive gifts of the first camellia, rose, snowdrop, or hellebore of the season, especially if they come "live" and later can be planted outside. Flower lovers particularly appreciate a new or unique plant, or something that you've proudly grown, say a favorite "old-fashioned" specie rose or a tree peony.

In the fall, a simple brown paper bag full of tulip bulbs tied with a sassy ribbon and a few cut tulips from the florist poking out from the top makes a terrific house gift for a gardener. This is a gift of promise and trust. A gift of bulbs or a collection of flower seeds in a basket nurtures a bond between the giver and receiver who must participate in the gift to realize the promise of beauty yet to come.

Such a gift has the potential to give of itself over and over through the coming months. Of course, the bulbs do have to be planted; maybe your generosity includes this service

WREATHS

One of the earliest arrangements of flowers for public events is the wreath. Formed in a perfect circle, the wreath is a mandala, a changeless geometric symbol constructed from natural flowers and foliage. In ancient times the Olympic victor was awarded a wreath of laurel, *Laurus nobilis* or sweet bay, the same plant we still use today to season our stews and soups. The modern term *bachelor*, associated with the baccalaureate degree, is derived from bacca-laureus, or laurel berry, through the French *bachelier*.

Throughout history, the ring of leaves and flowers was offered to honor heroes and mark special achievements. The circlets of rosebuds and baby's breath that crown the heads of flower girls at a wedding have their counterparts in the rings the bride and groom exchange. At the racetrack the winning horse is bedecked with a wreath or collar of flowers. At Christmas we hang wreaths of evergreen and holly, much like our pre-Christian ancestors, who used these plants to welcome the returning sun at the winter solstice. The wheel of the year was turning, bringing the promise of spring. Even in death we use the time-honored symbol of the wreath to bless the passing of our loved ones when their earthly lives have come full circle. With wreaths of laurel we honor dead heroes at war memorials. Like the serpent holding its tail, the wreath is a symbol of the continuing flow of life, death, and rebirth. It will probably endure forever.

An autumn house gift of a Chinese wooden tub is filled not with flowers but with apples, osage oranges, berries, and wild rose hips arranged in damp oasis and secured on short picks. A gift like this will last for weeks.

as well. If you choose to give prepared bulbs, say precooled narcissus, such as Chinese sacred-lilies, or hyacinths ready for forcing, your friends can begin to enjoy the gift while it's still winter. It is simple and satisfying to set the bulbs among pebbles or in a potting mix, add water, and store in a cool place. In no time, the roots will grow and expand, and the young shoots poke up. Later, in a measured sequence, your friends can bring the now-active bulbs to a cool, well-lit window where the entire magical process of growth unfolds before their eyes, and the promise of months before finally comes true in color and fragrance.

Along with ribbon and wrapping paper, flowers are appropriate as accessories for gifts. Whether it's a gardenia, a few stems of freesia, a full-blown garden rose, or even a nosegay of black-eyed Susans, butterfly weed, and dried seed heads from the country lane, the simple wildflowers you gather and send with the gift can mean much more than flowers from the florist. Suitability and your particular style are the important factors to consider.

There can be times when your gift is not really the surprise or as original as you had hoped for. When sweaters, sheets, or bath towels come in the store's box, they seem pretty standard. You can easily make the gift more memorable with flowers pulled through the bow. Or add a sprig of fragrant herbs inside the box, such as rosemary, lemon thyme, or scented geranium. By enclosing a sachet of potpourri inside the box, your prettily wrapped package can be transformed into something more surprising. When the package is opened, the fragrance adds to the enjoyment. Simple things, yes, but they convey more than a mass-produced greeting card, and they can become your special signature.

Flowers are also the perfect accompaniment for housewarming gifts and presents for newlyweds or newborn babies. Instead of just presenting a silver tray, salad bowl, or christening mug, add flowers. Imagine the pleasure of unwrapping a salad bowl to find it filled with fresh violets, a pitcher stuffed full of red tulips, or tiny pink rosebuds and lily of the valley in a christening mug. How do you keep flowers fresh inside a package? I suggest lining a bowl or platter with damp moss, and placing the violets on top. With a pitcher, arrange tulips in a bunch and tie as many as will just fit in the opening with string or riffia, add a little water, and set in a squat box with bubble wrap and masses of tissue paper as protection. Make sure to write *This Side Up* boldly on the outside of the box. A christening mug would require the same procedure. Keep the package cool until delivered. The flowers should remain fresh and fragrant until the gift is opened, even overnight.

For book lovers, include a pressed flower, such as a pansy, a sprig of lavender, or a red maple leaf, slipped between the pages or attached to a bookmark with a drop of glue. Not only the book but the new bookmark, signed with your special flower, will be a continual reminder of your thoughtfulness.

Last, don't forget plants as gifts, especially those that are aromatic, such as scented geraniums, lemon verbena, or lavender. Flowering plants are the easiest way to bring color to a friend's room, while the leaves of scented herbs can be used to add a pleasant fragrance to a bowl of dried petals or a linen drawer. Aromatic herbs, such as pineapple sage, basil, and lemon thyme, make excellent gifts for kitchen window boxes as well as herb gardens. Herbs today, even quite exotic ones, are becoming more common in most garden centers. The folklore that surrounds herbs might play quite nicely into what you want to say with a gift, but make sure you get your signals right. Thinking of herbs as gifts may recall the sad, mad Ophelia in *Hamlet*, who said: "There's rosemary, that's for remembrance; pray, love, remember: and there is pansies, that's for thoughts. There's fennel for you and columbines; there's rue for you and here's some for me; we may call it herb of grace o'Sundays. O! you must wear your rue with a difference. There's a daisy: I would give you some violets but they withered all when my father died."

113

What is a party cake without flowers? This Thanksgiving gift, baked by Sylvia Weinstock, is adorned with flowers made of sugar. For those whose culinary skills are not up to such an extravagant level, try placing a few real flowers atop the cake for a fresh look (just be sure they are nontoxic varieties).

THE
ESSENTIAL
GREEN

WE LIVE ON A GREEN PLANET, blessed by just the right amounts of sunlight and water. When I was about seven years old I observed a striking demonstration of this. I was in the isolation ward of the hospital recovering from an infectious fever and, like most young children, I was eager to get out and get on with my life. To help pass the time, I was given three large beans placed on a piece of wet flannel in a saucer. The dish sat on the windowsill where it received ample sunlight. I kept the flannel damp, and in a few days, before my very eyes I watched the beans sprout. First they sent out delicate roots; then the shell split open to expose two fat cotyledon, soon followed by a pair of tiny, perfect bright green leaves. The lesson was not lost on me: sunlight and water are the catalysts for providing the cycle of life and growth upon which all living things depend.

All my life I have been a heliophile, inspired by the magic energy of the sun. I marvel at the changing seasons of the year as all living things respond to the shifting amounts of water, heat, and light. I keenly observe the great chain of being, in which all the higher forms of life depend on chlorophyll. This miracle of photosynthesis is a remarkable process that has covered our planet with the wondrous complexity of botanical life. I marvel at the slow intricate development of a climax forest, the rapid recovery of nature after a forest fire, the basic role of greens in the food chain, as well as the life force hidden inside three dry beans.

I also observe, but with alarm, how humanity at the head of the food chain recklessly ignores the essential balance of nature. As the world's population swells, the forests that

LEFT: We can appreciate nature's design even in the underside of a green leaf.

PRECEDING PAGES: *Photograph by Horst.*

OPPOSITE: This arrangement is focused on green leaves—of Solomon's seal, varieties of hosta, fern fronds, and grass. The only flowers included are green-flowered foxglove and *Verbascum thapsus.*

provide so much of the earth's oxygen are being destroyed at an increasing rate each year. I wonder how long the earth can withstand this assault by society and technology. Can Mother Nature possibly rejuvenate herself as she seems to have done after other natural ecological disasters in the past? Taking care of our own backyards is at least a beginning.

As I watch the newly expanding leaves in the early spring, I am continually amazed at the diversity in these little shoots that produce oxygen for other living organisms. Some of them will become giant elephant ears, others long, delicate tendrils, some like green leather, some covered with fine hairs. Even the floating pond weed, barely one cell thick, does its small part in the ecosystem of a lake to provide the planet with oxygen. Nature sees to it that some kind of greenery thrives even in the most diverse climates. Compare the dense, thick, waxy foliage of the tropical rain forest with the solitary cactus growing in the intense sunlight of the desert, carefully preserving its supply of water within tough, leathery skin. Both are magnificent expressions of the irrepressible power of life.

In the vast world of plants and foliage, the single flower is merely a still point on an ever-turning cycle of living matter. Our appreciation of flowers should include the plants on which flowers grow and whose foliages are nature's complement to the limitless shapes and designs of the flowers themselves. At times the leaves alone create an arrangement when we need to bring the out-of-doors inside. Hosta leaves offer wonderful raw material with variegated fans of such green and white forms as *H. undulata medio-picta*, the rippled greenish blue of *H. sieboldiana*, or the gold of *H. "August Moon,"* plus some more than sixty species and new hybrids to choose from.

My favorite leaf forms include Solomon's seal, both green and variegated, ivy in an enormous variety of shapes and colors, exotic and hardy ferns, aphidistra, as well as blades of New Zealand flax (*Phormium tenax*) and the dramatic leaf

A green place in a city or town is always enjoyable. The white *Wisteria floribunda* "Alba" is a natural canopy.

forms of such perennials as mahonia, macleaya, aruncus, fatsia, and artemisia. In spring I cut branches of the lime green flowers of the Norway maple, or the flaky bracts of elm. The greenish white flowers of the native dogwood, the highlight of spring here in the Northeast, make statements of utter naturalness when used in the right setting. Or they can provide an impressive backdrop and setting for the most brilliant colors of the garden in large arrangements. And sometimes I reverse the technique, making greenery the main component of an arrangement garnished with a few white or even green flowers.

I have always been fascinated by the wonderful assortment of flowers that are naturally green. These include the lime green alchemilla, (especially *A. mollis*), the apple green of flowering tobacco (*Nicotiana affinis*), the green zinnia called "Envy," the spired Bells of Ireland (*Molucella laevis*), fragrant mignonette, and *Amaranthus viridus* with its trailing chenille plumes. Other naturally green flowers are the large and miniature forms of gladioli, green flushed tulips (such as Greenland), many euphorbia varieties, the green calla lily (such as *Zantedeschia* "Green Goddess"), certain varieties of chrysanthemums (Shamrock), *Helleborus corsicus*, and *H. foetidissima*, not to mention artichokes, and even a green rose—

the ancient *Rosa viridiflora*, or Green China rose. Imaginative use of green materials alone can create, in their subtle way, an effect that is as stunning as any combination of the most eye-catching colors.

In choosing greenery to punctuate an arrangement of cut flowers or to be the unique focal point of a design, there are many interesting textures and shapes to consider: showy succulents, such as aloe or echeveria, even the rosettes of "hens and chicks," delicate ferns, ornamental grasses, ivies, rushes and reeds, as well as pads of mosses and lichens. A branch of silver birch adorned with fresh young leaves in spring can be used as imaginatively as a similar branch of liquid ambar or maple a few months later when the leaves have turned to autumn colors. Cultivating many of these different greens or scavenging for them in the wild increases the raw materials for many arrangements and offers a challenge to express yourself with a limited palette of colors.

Ferns are an excellent choice for bringing exotic greenery indoors. They are some of the oldest surviving plant forms on earth. Without flowers or seeds for reproduction, they manufacture spores that drop from their fronds, become asexually active, and create the next generation of ferns. Ferns grow easily outdoors in shady, cool places; they can thrive in both mountains and jungles. In New Zealand alone there are more than 150 varieties, from the minute, delicate, filmy ferns that grow on the moist forest floor up to giant tree ferns fifty feet high. Many families can be grown in summer as outdoor pot plants in filtered light with the soil kept damp to satisfy their preference for humidity. Indoors, ferns should be kept away from heaters and radiators. They need good light and enjoy an occasional misting. The Boston fern is the most common house fern and grows well in bright light. A little organic plant food from time to time, plus the constant trimming of old fronds will encourage growth. The duvallia, or rabbit's foot fern, is an ideal house plant that needs very little sun and grows well in baskets or pots. While it appreciates the humidity of a kitchen windowsill, it can withstand long droughts and even shed its leaves. But because of its furry foot or storage rhizome, it is easily revived with renewed watering. The elegant maidenhair fern, a popular item in Victorian homes, cannot endure hot, dry conditions but does well in cool, unheated rooms with the temperature in the 50s–60s in winter and on shady porches in the summer. And its hardy garden relatives, such as *Adiantum pedatum*, do wonderfully in the woodland soil of the Northeast.

Repotting ferns is best done in the spring. Simply knock the fern and its root mass out of the pot. Cut all the old fronds back to the crown, and shake the soil off the roots. With a sharp knife, cut the fibrous mat of roots into either halves or quarters. Saw right through the bound root system. Ease the roots apart, trim a little, and repot each clump in a mixture of one-half peat moss and one-half sifted compost to which you have added a teaspoon of Electra or

119

We can appreciate flowering plants even when they are not in bloom. Fronting the meadow are Chinese fir, *Cunninghamia* *lanceolata glauca*, hardy cactus, *Opuntia compressa*, Colorado blue spruce, and immature flowers of sedum.

HORTICULTURAL THERAPY

Flowers in a doctor's waiting room are not solely decorative. Nature has always been and continues to be the great healer. The calming flow of fish and plants in an aquarium has proven beneficial for hospital patients, particularly the emotionally disturbed. And flowers growing in a garden or window box have been shown to have a healing effect on the sick, the lonely, and the disabled.

Each seed, bulb, stalk, leaf, blossom says nothing more than, "Admire me! I am full of life! I am yours!" Working in a garden an hour a day, potting a plant that has outgrown its container, or arranging a bouquet for the evening meal has tremendous therapeutic effect. Living things that need our assistance draw out our gentler selves. We become more loving and considerate. Hopefully, the curative effect of working with nature can draw our minds away from the competitive work world and the depressing news stories of violence and hardship. Flowers capture our fantasies about life at its best, at its healthiest. We plant seeds and watch things grow; life returns, and with it hope. The amaryllis bulb sends forth a shoot, the bud appears, then a succession of glorious red blossoms—and we instinctively feel better.

A display and working greenhouse attached to the Howard Rusk Institute at New York University Hospital in Manhattan provides a practical hands-on opportunity for patients who are able to get around and get their hands dirty. Their spirits are lifted caring for flowers and plants throughout the year.

organic plant food and a little coarse sand or perlite. Water well and set the new pots outside in the shade or under a tree where they will receive filtered light.

Terrariums are another way to bring nature indoors. In and out of favor since Victorian times, they continue to make great gifts for children or the homebound since they offer a self-contained miniature world of mystery and imagination. They were first developed from the Wardian cases used by nineteenth-century plant explorers to transport their exotic plants from China and South America back to the gardens of Europe. Basically a trunk with glass panels that could be opened on the sides for ventilation, Wardian cases kept the plants protected and alive on the ships' open decks. The new floral attractions at London's Crystal Palace Exhibition in the 1850s inspired a whole generation of plant lovers to attempt to grow tropical plants indoors and to cultivate ferns, palms, and the small plants that thrive under glass domes; hence the development of the terrarium. Miniature ferns, mosses, and tiny flowering plants, such as dwarf gesneriads and orchids that relish high humidity, can create a veritable forest floor in miniature. Insect-catching swamp plants, such as the Venus's-flytrap, and pre–ice age survivors, like the Selaginella family and lycopodium, or prince's-pine, can delight children while teaching them about a natural ecosystem with growing things in competitive balance.

Also harking back to Victorian days are the statuesque palms seen in hotel foyers and conservatories. Still prominent is the classic kentia palm that graced many nineteenth-century parlors. Curiously, this slow-growing, graceful dark green palm is found only on tiny Lord Howe Island in the southwest Pacific (and is correctly called *Howea forsteriana*); yet it has become a standard element for interior design all over the world. The well-known areca palm is inexpensive, long-lasting, and will thrive on a bright porch. Most palms, however, require only medium to low light and prefer to dry out slightly between regular watering. They must not be allowed to stand in water. Feed them once a month or every six weeks with organic plant food (weakfish emulsion is ideal); and, if possible, take them outside and hose them down occasionally to simulate a good rain shower. This keeps their leaves free of dust and discourages such parasites as red spider.

Probably the best-known house and office plants are members of the dracaena family. They are a hardy group, requiring little water, and can somehow survive in dark apartments and interior rooms that get little natural light. Probably the most handsome is the variegated *Dracaena warneckii* with green-and-white striped leaves. The commercial association with restaurants and banks has made the dracaena seem like a cliché, but I think if used thoughtfully in the right pot or setting, it has great potential, especially as part of a grouping. Keep it clean, remove old leaves, fertilize it two or three times a year, and turn it at intervals throughout

the year to get the best light. It happens that dracaena can sometimes repay for modest care with a head of fragrant, waxy, cream-colored stars.

Other favorite houseplants include African violets and many other gesneriads, orchids, bromeliads, spathiphyllum, and the semi-succulent hoya. The latter is excellent in hanging baskets or planters and can be trained to grow over hooks to create a living valance around windows. A member of the milkweed family asclepia, hoya has waxy leaves, sometimes splashed with silver, that are very decorative and long-lasting.

Of the flowering plants, orchids form the largest family in the natural world, intriguing us with strange and bizarre flowers in every color and size. In fact, the mystery and romance associated with these plants set them apart from all others, since they were first exhibited over 150 years ago. The fascination with orchids derives from several characteristics: their growth in remote locales in exotic countries; their trophy status among plant hunters; their odd growth habits, perched in a branch with aerial roots; their often amazing fragrance; the extraordinary variety of devices they use to attract and trick pollinating insects; as well as a high price tag and a reputation for being difficult to grow. Today, however, inexpensive orchids unknown to our grandparents are available at every garden center, and given the right care, many varieties can grow happily in an average home.

Among the best-loved is the so-called moth orchid, or phalaenopsis, with arching sprays of very long-lasting white or pink flowers that bloom throughout the year. Easiest to grow for many people are those of the cymbidium group. As a mature plant, cymbidiums produce many spikes of bloom—even in winter if kept in a cool garden room or greenhouse. The extravagant white or lavender flower of the cattleya can thrive in a steamy bathroom, while the sensual flowers of a hybrid lady's slipper, or paphiopedilum, could do nicely on the kitchen windowsill. In the entire world of

The dramatic blue-green leaves of the summer-blooming *Macleaya cordata* "Plume poppy" demand a place in the garden. The foliage is really the star here—the flowers are almost incidental.

BELOW: Ornamental grasses are very easy to grow in most climates.

OPPOSITE: In the corner of a room, a dramatic spot of green is created using trails of *Amaranthus viridus*, the flowers and foliage of oak leaf hydrangea, Algerian ivy, hosta leaves, and grasses.

122

orchids, I especially treasure one that grows wild in the woods here in the Northeast, the pink lady's slipper (*Cypripedium acaule*). But wherever I discover them—in the cloud forests of Costa Rica, in the foothills of the Himalayas, or even on the forest floor of my native New Zealand—I am always amazed by their special diversity and ability to survive. I must warn newcomers to the world of orchids that they can become addictive. Many neophytes begin with one humble plant in the window, soon become hooked, and before you know it, they have invested in greenhouses and are entering local orchid shows! A word to the wise is sufficient.

Most herbs do not make satisfying houseplants, and I have never known a windowsill herb garden to fulfill the extravagant promises of the seed catalogs. To be realistic, herbs need good soil, plenty of sun, and vigorous growing conditions. In any garden with good light and ventilation they develop more stamina and flavor than those raised in the confinement of a pot. Some herbs—cat mint, lemon sorrel, horseradish, sage, and thyme—are hardy perennials, while others—basil, parsley, chives, and coriander—must be started from fresh seed each spring. Most herbs are a summer crop in the Northeast, but some can be cut back and potted indoors during the winter where, given good light, they make admirable house plants: a rosemary bush, a bay tree, or a scented geranium are a few examples.

Fresh herbs in salads and soups or sprinkled over cold fish in the summer enhance the simplest meal. I also add garden herbs to summer teas and punches. But we should not overlook the nonculinary uses for herbs, such as centerpieces for the breakfast table or added to other flower groups as potpourri, and as borders along the walk near the kitchen

door where they will also be handy for cooking. Using herbs in potpourri is a tradition that goes back to the Middle Ages, when they were used as natural deodorants, liberally strewn throughout rooms and hallways to compensate for the rich mix of human, animal, and vegetable odors that characterized medieval life. Today the natural fragrances of lemon verbena, rosemary, rose geranium, and lavender still find a welcome place in linen drawers and closets and closed-up rooms. Try keeping a sachet of herbs in the car to sweeten the air shared with cigarette smokers.

Window boxes provide a home or apartment with that vital greenery that has both an indoor and outdoor quality, appreciated by their owners as well as the neighbors. For many apartment dwellers a summer window box can be a kind of signature and personal statement to those one may never meet face to face. In its humble way, a window box helps break down the anonymity of urban life. Although a window box presents a very limited area for cultivation, it is amazing what can be grown in one. I favor trailing plants such as vinca, ivy, cascading verbena, blue lantana, and trailing rosemary. Of course, marigolds, geraniums, nierembergias, petunias, herbs, and scented geraniums can also be included. The easy care and maintenance of window boxes appeals to many people for whom a full garden would be too burdensome. It is not much harder than caring for goldfish or a canary. Flowers in window boxes, however, need daily watering and regular feeding with a supplement, such as Miracle-Gro, since nutrients in a limited amount of soil need replacement and a sunny exposure quickly dries out the soil. By deadheading and cutting back lanky growth, a windowsill garden can bloom heartily up to the first frost. For apartments on the shady side of a building there are plant varieties that will do just fine: coleus, impatiens, begonia, ivy geranium, browallia, and lobelia, along with such trailing foliage plants as variegated vinca major, grape ivy or other members of the cissus family, and wandering Jew.

Cactus and all the great variety of succulents are examples of extreme specialization in plants that have evolved to withstand prolonged drought and harshly sunny conditions. In modern interiors with central heating and dry atmosphere, they can do quite well with just a little water and plenty of natural light. Overwatering will quickly kill them. I personally find their rigid, static forms out of place in my house, but as a variety of exotic plant sculpture they can be just the right addition for the steel, glass, and stone interiors of many public places. Lobbies, conference centers, and well-lit office waiting rooms have utilized cactus and succulents to great advantage.

The bonsai is another example of extreme specialization in nature. Dwarf trees do appear naturally in the wild, the best-known example in America being bristlecone pine (*Pinus aristata*) in the mountains of Nevada. As some of the oldest living plants on the continent, they have adapted to the extreme lack of moisture and poor soil, intense winds and sunlight, as well as great fluctuations in temperature.

In a green Chinese bowl, a purist's look is achieved with spikes of *Yucca filamentosa*, stalks of Egyptian onion, and flowers of *Alchemilla mollis* with hardy maidenhair fern and a variety of hosta leaves.

The trunk and limbs of a natural bonsai acquire the twisted, gnarled look of great age, in striking contrast to its fresh green needles.

Along with their great skill in ikebana, the Japanese have perfected the art of "creating" bonsai trees by skillfully cutting, bending, and wiring young plants, pruning the roots and tips each year, and replanting in low trays so that the ultimate effect is a small antique tree that appears to have withstood many years of weathering on some remote cliffside. In a sense, the bonsai is the "pet plant" par excellence: trained to be and do just what its owner desires. Understanding their special needs is the key to their survival. Deciduous bonsai plants need a full natural season of growth and should be kept protected outside during the winter in a cold frame. On the other hand, the tropical species, such as citrus, hibiscus, or ficus, continue to make new growth and require a warm environment all year. Healthy, well-maintained bonsai are exciting to see, whether grown individually in private homes or exhibited in great numbers at public gardens, such as the unique collection at the Brooklyn Botanic Gardens.

Full-size indoor trees, such as ficus, hibiscus, oleander, and camellia, each have their special needs, but given sufficient light can become perfect houseplants offering a great return for loving care. Ficus, for example, can almost dry out between regular waterings. It appreciates occasional feeding from March until October, and if not outdoors for the summer, it should be turned so that the entire tree receives light. When pinched and pruned regularly, it will grow to fit the space and amount of light available; in other words, it will not thrive above the window in the darker corners of the ceiling where branches and leaves would be sparse and sickly.

An orange or lemon tree appreciates the maximum amount of time outside in the summer to stimulate natural growth, but it should be brought indoors as the days begin to shorten and kept in a cool yet bright room to rest, with

FRAGRANCE

One of the most endearing qualities of flowers is their perfume. This unique trait is the result of light and temperature's effect on a growing plant. It is also how the plants attract pollinators: bees, flies, moths, butterflies, birds, even some animals. Some flowers are more aromatic during the evening: tuberose, night-scented stock, night-blooming jasmine, and many orchids. The warmth of midday enhances the perfume of wallflower, stock, and buddleia—to attract butterflies. In nature, it is interesting to note that large, showy flowers, such as hollyhock, sunflower, zinnia, and hydrangea, lack a strong fragrance, depending instead on their flamboyant form and color to attract "suitors" (lilies and peonies are the notable exceptions to the rule). And very small flowers, like violets, daphne, pinks, or sweet spice bush (*Clethra alnifolia*), are often intensely fragrant, as if in compensation.

Through breeding, man has upset this to some degree. I often hear the sad complaint that "modern" or hybrid roses have lost their scent. This put-down of the new varieties is not entirely warranted when you consider the lovely perfume of such current favorites as French Lace, Fragrant Cloud, Friendship, Don Juan, and, of course, Perfume Delight. Among the newly fashionable English roses of the talented nurseryman David Austin, the fragrant appeal of their ancient ancestors has been retained.

The perception of a flower's particular scent differs from person to person. What may seem seductive to one may be overpowering to another, particularly with such strongly scented flowers as tuberose, gardenia, or night-scented jasmine.

reduced watering and no feeding over the winter. Hibiscus, oleander, and camellia also can grow outdoors on the patio or porch during the summer and be brought inside for the winter. The hibiscus sets new buds in the fall and will often flower all winter in a pool house or even the living-room window during the short days of the year. The camellia also flowers during the winter in a cool environment—it's quite tough enough to thrive in a garage, mud room, or other unheated room where there is good light and the temperature drops to the low 40s.

In our quest for the perfect environment for ourselves and our plants, human ingenuity has devised artificial means of light to replace or supplement the natural energy from the sun. Growlights provide almost the full spectrum of sunlight by means of incandescent lamps and fluorescent tubes. Their greatest value to me is for starting seeds in flats during the winter months. They are not particularly attractive, and many people keep their "growing shelves" in the basement or garage. The lightweight frame units are adjustable to keep the light source at the proper distance from the plants as they grow. Small orchids and African violets, as examples, thrive happily in this alternative source of light.

The use of high-intensity grow-lights in public buildings to supplement sunlight makes it possible for unexpected trees and plants of all sizes and species to survive in places that would seem hostile to plant life. (The extraordinary palm court of New York's World Financial Center provides visible proof of this.) And thus we provide that vital touch of nature—alive and green—in our hermetically sealed, totally artificial environments. No more than a touch, of course, for there can really be no substitute for the miraculous power of sunlight—either for plants or for humans.

Going beyond the vocabulary of roses and carnations can be interesting. The male flowers of the South African silver tree *Leucadendron argentea* are arresting enough by themselves.

SOURCES
FOR
FLOWERS

BELOW: The flower district of any major city is the place to see fresh flowers and plants.

PRECEDING PAGES:
Photograph by Horst.

RIGHT: Flowers are sold almost everywhere: the supermarket, at stands on the highway, and even at delis throughout Manhattan. Before you buy, take a look at the stock to make sure it's fresh.

AN INVETERATE AND COMPULSIVE flower arranger, I consider the garden my primary source and grow a wide range of flowers in specific colors. As well as their key role in the landscape, the different garden areas provide the colors, forms, and textures that I rely on for the arrangements in the house throughout the growing season. Another source of raw materials is nature herself, along back-country roads or streams, out in the fields or meadows, or hidden deep in the woodlands. For commercial work where large quantities are required I depend on the wholesale resources in New York City and the wonderful local nurseries on Long Island.

The Cutting Garden

Planning and maintaining a cutting garden is a challenging exercise, for there are always many new varieties to try out. From the winter days when we pour over seed catalogs, dreaming of all the possibilities, to the heart of summer

where we are managing a full-blooming yard, the gardener is happily engaged in the constantly changing scene of growth and color. A garden is a dynamic thing, on the move, pushing the limits by continuously replacing itself with new growth. From year to year, the same plot of land can be planted in different and exciting ways. While I rely on my favorite performers and replant the successful crop, I also like to experiment and try something different. Boring is the gardener who takes the conservative approach and replants the same garden year after year. That's why I carefully scan the catalogs during the winter months as well as take a pad and pencil with me when visiting public gardens or arboretums to see what's greener over the fence.

A cutting garden is never really finished, even after the rows are laid out, the seeds planted, and the first tender shoots break through the soil. It becomes a seasonal process rather than an accomplished fact: a succession of crops, a recycling of space. Even as a beginner, you have to consider performance and growing schedules so there is not too much overplanting or bad timing. For example, prudent shepherding of facilities should leave room for both the lily and the tomato plants, and parsley as well. Sweet peas will give way by the end of June to rows of dahlias or snapdragons that will be hearty and colorful right up to the first frost. It is important also to know how different plants affect the soil. All the legumes, sweet peas, beans, or "sugar snaps," for example, enhance nitrogen production in the soil, so when their life cycle is over in June, you can dig the remains into the ground to help fertilize the autumn crops. Tulips should not be grown in the same ornamental beds for more than two years as subsequent plantings can become susceptible to "tulip fire," a disfiguring virus.

Laying out a garden requires creative use of available space and a healthy respect for the unique features of the land and the natural conditions, such as sunlight, shade, water runoff, protection from wind and animals, and so

forth. When you come right down to it, a garden is a matter of personal taste realized through a gardener's individual ability and needs, and nature's cooperation. In general, however, easy access to water is a must because proper irrigation can be a major key to a successful garden. A north-south layout is important so that maximum sunlight will shine down the rows of plants as the sun swings overhead and slightly south each day. Keep the play of sunlight in mind when determining the location of individual plants. In a perennial border, for example, taller plants should be placed north of shorter ones so that they don't block sunlight. Six- to seven-foot dahlias should be planted behind two- to three-foot *Salvia farinacea*.

I highly recommend mulching as a major time- and labor-saving aid in both the vegetable and cut-flower garden. It helps to keep moisture in the ground and eliminate weed growth. As you apply mulch each year, the garden becomes increasingly weed-free. Mulching the garden beds may require a little extra work and expense up front, but in the long run it will save a lot of time and frustration.

Dry salt hay cut from tidal marshes makes an excellent mulch because, unlike baled hay from the fields and meadows,

The smallest patch of earth, a window box, or an acre of land can be a source for cut flowers and foliage.

it does not contain weed seeds that will immediately sprout in your tomato patch. You don't need to import weeds; the indigenous variety are sufficient, thank you! Other materials that can be used as mulches include seaweed, shredded cedar bark, cocoa hulls, used hops from a brewery, your own shredded leaves, and grass clippings. All these are organic and biodegradable, aesthetically pleasing, and can even lend color and texture to the garden layout. I suggest that you extend the mulch a bit beyond the fence to control weeds or grass under the fence itself. This will keep the garden tidier.

Layers of newspaper make an excellent sterile mulch between rows. They can be applied early and quickly, and then covered with grass clippings as the summer lawn takes off. I tend not to recommend black plastic (except for commercial gardens). Although it is practical and effective, it is aesthetically unappealing. Of course as a ground cover, like newspaper, it can be hidden by a generous cover of wood chips. Pierce a good number of holes in the plastic to allow passage of water, and it will be perfect for a newly planted border of evergreen shrubs.

A sturdy, attractive fence will enhance almost any garden. Flowers and vegetables are at the mercy of rodents, pets, and children and deserve some form of protection. A good fence will also frame your garden and give it a neat, self-contained look that imposes a little order on those crazy rows. A traditional post-and-rail fence is ideal because you can easily remove rails if you need to move in equipment, such as rototillers, wheelbarrows, or a truckload of farm manure. The open post-and-rail design allows sunlight and air to circulate freely, which a closed board or stockade fence will not, and it provides a natural support for your favorite climbing plants: the old-fashioned annual *Mina lobata*, clematis, morning glories, and roses. To keep out rabbits and other varmints, staple heavy chicken wire down from the lower rail (and on the gate!) and about six to eight inches into the ground so that hungry predators can't burrow under.

THE FLOWER SHOW

The earliest flower shows, in the middle of the seventeenth century, were modest gatherings of amateurs who met to hold feasts and to display "special florists' flowers," which included carnation, tulip, anemone, hyacinth, and my favorite, the auricula. Today a flower show anywhere in the world can draw a large audience, whether it is a display of cascade and bonsai chrysanthemums beneath the walls of Matsumoto Castle in Japan, or an exhibit of tropical orchids in the Sydney Botanical Gardens in Australia, or the best U.S. shows in San Francisco, Seattle, Cinncinnati, Atlanta, and Philadelphia.

The world's most illustrious flower show is probably the annual extravaganza of the Royal Horticultural Society held in May on the grounds of the Royal Hospital, Chelsea, in London. Now in its eighty-seventh year, it covers twenty-three acres, both outdoors and under marquees on the banks of the Thames. It never fails to deliver on its promise of offering the best: classic garden flowers, like six-foot delphiniums, oceans of sweet peas, bright or more fragrant roses and carnations, collections of orchids, miniature alpine plants, and exotica from all corners of the globe.

Because the Chelsea show is so famous, it can be tough getting tickets unless you belong to the Royal Horticultural Society or know someone who does. But if you are in London in July, try the big and wonderful Hampton Court Flower Show, with more of everything in the glorious setting of Henry VIII's Hampton Court Palace.

PRECEDING PAGES: Your local flower shop can be a gold mine of fresh materials and sound advice. Special flowers and plants are easily ordered. (*Photograph at left by Horst.*)

ABOVE: Farm stands in the countryside are a summer source for freshly picked flowers. Often one is allowed out into the fields to cut a handsome selection.

The "right" fence is one that adds a gracious architectural role to the landscape. It can suggest a pleasant formality without being intimidating. A gate at each end of the garden says, "Come in and wander through; the garden is not off-limits." I suggest that gardeners construct a temporary fence for a summer garden if they object to a permanent structure that would alter the look of their lawn or yard year-round. A fence consisting of metal or wooden fence posts strung with chicken wire, plus a gate somewhere along the way, is probably sufficient to keep out dogs and footballs. It's inexpensive and can be removed and rolled up for winter, when the ground is turned over or sown with winter rye to await the new season. If keeping out deer is a problem, a serious eight-foot-high cyclone netting or electrical fence might be the only solution.

A fence can also be used creatively to provide vertical space. If the ground area is limited by geography, a gardener might plan a greater yield by planting climbing plants along fences and trellises. When I lay out a garden, I think three-dimensionally and try to devise a setting for the tall climbers: honeysuckle, trumpet vine, clematis, or roses. Even the temporary measure of tall canes attached to the fence posts can create a wonderful screen for such annuals as blue morning glory or the purple cobea vine. A high, wire tennis-court fence can become a perfect jungle gym for a combination of climbing New Dawn, Tiffany, or Peace roses, deliciously laced with pink and lavender clematis for a seasonal screen of color where it is most appreciated.

Take a little extra care in laying out and lining pathways. Define the paths and walkways with a mulch that contrasts with that used in the beds. In traditional Long Island gardens, for example, crushed shells from the local oyster beds are a popular native material for walks. In other parts of the country, wood chips and pine or cedar bark are widely used. I would strongly recommend, however, that when planning gravel mulch for a pathway, you line the walk with steel or heavy vinyl edging to prevent the gravel from moving into the lawn or planted area. Paths should always be wide enough to allow for moving around when weeding, watering, cutting, or trucking the wheelbarrow in to gather crops. A sundial, birdbath, bench, or elevated birdhouse at the intersection of paths can create a sentimental centerpoint for the garden and provide an aesthetic focus.

With the longer days comes the spring surge, and controlling growth and keeping the burgeoning garden in check means pinching back the growing annuals to encourage root growth and a stockier branching plant. This is also the time to stake or support plants so they can handle wind and rain. There are many methods for staking different plants. While opinions vary on the aesthetics of staking, it ideally does its job without being seen.

Sweet peas, for example, can be well supported by a thicket of birch twigs beneath a teepee of rigid bamboo poles. They take hold with their eager tendrils and haul themselves up to the sunlight in record time. A row of growing cosmos, however, is best contained between a parallel row of strong stakes, four to five feet apart and at least four feet high, cross-laced with garden twine. Strong winds can destroy a stand of these dependable, long-blooming favorites, but not if you take the precaution of staking them. The supports make them easier to pick and the growth soon hides them. A row or bed of lower-growing annuals, such as blue salvia, cornflowers, Shirley poppies, or nigellas, are best supported by a loose cage of twigs or branches set among the young plants. Prunings from maple, birch, beech, or even dogwood, salvaged from the rubbish heap, are fine. Set the branches firmly in the ground and they will soon be covered by the plant whose light bulk is easily supported by this natural framework. A strong simple stake will suffice for the sunflower, but the clump of delphinium requires a circling

ring of three or four stakes with a cross web of horizontal twine to support the brittle stems. A handy aid to support taller perennials is also available from most garden-supply catalogs or garden centers. It's an enameled circular grid of crossed wires on legs of different heights which provides a "grow through" support that really does the job, minimizing staking in the border and, of course, reusable each season.

Perennials

The backbone of the flower lover's garden will certainly be the dependable perennials, from the early blooming dicentra and lily of the valley to the late aster and chrysanthemum that challenge frost. From shade to full sun, in dappled woodland or brilliant seaside, here are the plants that furnish the ultimate variety in all the colors you love, no matter what they may be.

Probably because of the care involved, perennial gardens went out of favor for years, but now it seems a renaissance is under way. American culture, with its love of novelty, constant change, and lack of commitment, may have discouraged the perennial garden in the English tradition, but with recent efforts by garden clubs, the new breed of supply companies and—most noticeably—books, magazines, and plant-and-seed catalogs, it seems American gardeners are hurrying to catch up. Today the volume of orders with perennial nurseries is greater than ever. It should come as no surprise, however, that a perennial garden is not carefree. It requires the same meticulous maintenance and commitment as a seasonal garden, and since it is a permanent feature of the landscape with a year-round profile, careful planning is a large part of your investment.

My perennial gardens are contained in sunny terraced beds on sloping banks as well as under tall trees that form the wooded hollow where my home lies. It doesn't matter whether your land is flat or hilly, sunny or shady; there are perennials today for most ecological niches. However, when

Many botanical gardens and arboretums have garden centers of their own where one can buy fresh greenhouse plants. They may also offer courses where you can learn to grow your own flowers and plants under pristine conditions.

WHAT TO DO
WITH ONE
HUGE DAHLIA

I grow dahlias in rows in the sunny vegetable garden because, although I am personally not fond of them, these remarkable hybrid descendants of mountain flowers found in Mexico and Central America thrive through a long season in wonderful colors and staggering variety. The huge plate-size dahlia offers a challenge to a flower arranger since it is top-heavy and looks all wrong in a vase. I am often asked, "What can I do with it?"

One possible use is as a centerpiece for the dining table. Choose a shallow bowl or vegetable dish with a high enough side wall to hold water, and anchor a needlepoint holder in the center with floral adhesive. As a dramatic setting, arrange large leaves, such as colorful hosta, artichoke, ornamental curly kale, or the silver dusty miller. Sear the end of the dahlia stem with a match to aid water absorption, and impale the flower in the center of the arrangement. The leaves may last two weeks, and the conversation-piece dahlia may be changed every three to four days if it fades.

creating a perennial bed or border, even a modest one, for a succession of bloom in a controlled color pattern, choose the plants with care and an area with maximum sunlight. This is especially true if the border is planned to yield a succession of cutting flowers. Here I suggest you include annuals and flowering bulbs to fill out the season's supply.

The entire garden of a friend I greatly admired contained only her favorite pinks and lavenders, but for me the excitement of other colors is a must. I vote for variety of color and form. If you are troubled by the challenge of too many colors, groups of fresh white can calm and unify the diverse elements in a mixed perennial border, and fortunately there is a substantial selection of whites to choose from. In fact, all the principal perennial plant families usually have white varieties. Think of the traditionally blue or lavender delphiniums, for example; the Galahad strains offer their elegant white spikes of bloom with a striking black "bee" in the center. The native snakeroot, *Cimicifuga*, is at home in shady corners and at the back of the garden. The variety *C. racemosa* blooms in August, while the equally vigorous *C.* "White Pearl" shows up in the late days of October. White summer phlox, such as Fujiyama, White Admiral, and the delightful Phlox maculata "Miss Lingard," offer what I think are the whitest imaginable flowers. The balloon flower, platycodon from Japan, is a reliable mid- to late summer bloomer usually chosen for its wide, open, lavender-blue cup, but also available in equally appealing pale pink and white forms. Peonies, of course, come in single and double white forms while many range through the cream to palest pink shades. The hardy New England aster, *A. novi-belgii*, has tall and low-growing white forms; Mt. Everest and White Fairy are two, but a cousin, Boltonia "Snowbank," almost outflowers them with its generous display. Astilbe, which is a durable hardy plant that is quite happy in partial shade, offers many tall and short varieties in white. I particularly like the ostrich plume type, *A.* "Prof van der Wielen," with

If you plan your own cutting garden, make sure to plant an abundant crop that will last a full season and can be used in many arrangements.

its nodding spike and handsome foliage, while I grow and recommend the prolific, fluffy white Deutschland.

A taller but very similar plant and an early summer favorite of mine is *Aruncus dioicus*, or goats-beard, an unforgettable beauty in bloom. Starting out a fresh greeny white, the flowers fade prettily to cream as they mature, and even when these are removed the foliage holds—a cover for the white lilies to follow. *Lilium regale*, brought to the West from China by E. H. Wilson in the early 1900s, is a richly perfumed white lily that is justly famous. The Easter lily, *L. longiflorum*, is very much at home in my garden as well, along with two newer introductions from the Oregon bulb growers, the white tiger lily and the sensational white auratum hybrid called Casa Blanca. Favorite among white lilies, however, is probably the Madonna lily (*Lilium candidum*) — elegant, pure white, and with a clear and beautiful fragrance.

Don't overlook the Siberian forms of white iris, such as *Iris siberica* "Snow Queen," and the many bearded or German irises with their brief but glorious display. White oriental poppies, notably *Papauer orientale* "Marshall van der

Glotz" and "White King," and white yucca flowers tower in the hillside garden; white lilacs and white buddleia screen the compost heap. Spiky clumps of white lupine, foxglove, and the low-growing arabis, iberis, and white trailing phlox line the pathways. Without any effort, you can probably also think of white shasta daisies, roses, violas, and hydrangreas. One could certainly fill a border or two with just white perennial plants to bloom throughout the season.

It's a pointless exercise to choose a favorite cutting flower. I love what's just coming out on any day; but if pushed, I'll admit that for me the peony is queen and tops my list. Peonies are at once the synthesis of all that is beautiful in flowers and come in a totally satisfying range of color, usually accompanied by a variety of subtle fragrances and extraordinary silken petals. I love them all from the tiny tree peony (*Peonia delavayi*) in shades of green or copper to the stately long-stemmed, herbaceous, shell-pink "Baroness Schroeder." The aristocrat among peonies is certainly the tree peony, whose woody shrubs produce the largest, most dazzling silken single or double flowers of indescribable loveliness. If you don't own any, invest in a masterpiece and grow a rare surprise. I recommend that extra herbaceous peonies be grown in rows in the vegetable garden for cutting, as well as occupying significant spots in the perennial border. There can never be too many peonies, either to cut or simply to enjoy in the garden.

Old Favorites

As a source of flowers for arrangements and as colorful additions to the garden, I encourage flower lovers not to overlook the "old favorites" that ironically have fallen out of fashion. The dahlia, gladiolus, and carnation seem to head this list. I think I can understand what makes so many people dislike these serviceable and useful flowers. Invariably when I question clients about why they are so adamant about my not using these once-popular flowers in arrangements, their answers indicate strong memories or associations that they find at odds with their current lifestyle or living room. The year-round supply of inexpensive gladioli, for example, provides the staple in funeral designs, and for many people that is the major association with this flower. But gladioli may deserve a place in the garden.

Gladioli can transform the prosaic rows of a vegetable garden into a more pleasing and visually interesting spot. Years ago in New Zealand I inherited a box of gladioli bulbs that I didn't want to throw out and yet they didn't fit the plans I made for the terraced flower beds. So I planted them in staggered sequence in the vegetable garden, between rows of lettuce, peas, and carrots. Working in that sunny garden was always an enjoyable experience surrounded by their bright colors; and I always had flowers as well as salad to take when invited to friends' homes to dine. To this day I still associate gladioli with the happy days of working in that vegetable garden high above the bay in Napier.

Gladioli are available in an enormous range of sizes and colors. Particularly attractive are the miniature and dwarf forms whose spiky little flowers are useful in a gathering of mixed garden flowers. In mild climates like California, where gladioli bulbs can be left to naturalize in the ground, I recommend a specie form, *Gladioli tristis*, a small beige-and-green hooded flower with a subtle fragrance. In the Northeast these must be winterized in pots in a cool greenhouse, along with other such desirable bulbs as *Nerines lachenalia* and crinum lilies.

I also spring to the defense of dahlias. They can offer wonderful variety and infuse the garden with their color over a long period, growing happily with very little encouragement. The more you cut them, the more they thrust out new flowers and provide an amazing supply of blooms from summer through fall, with their strongest flowering occurring up to the first frost. Plant them in the vegetable garden where they'll grow vigorously and create a charming contrast to rows of lettuce or cabbage; or use them in the flower garden

ABOVE: Garden centers are the ultimate resource for flowers and plants: annuals, perennials, shrubs, herbs, trees, spring bulbs. The proper supplies and tools, garden furniture and containers, and good advice are also offered.

OPPOSITE: This beautiful garden in Vermont illustrates how a well-planned garden can provide endless joy. Choose a place for a garden wisely, making sure that the area for planting is well drained and gets enough sunlight during the day. You may want to plant for year-round enjoyment, so consider the sequence of the seasons before proceeding. Most of all, only plant what you can handle in terms of space— you can always expand the garden later.

or along a walk or wall. The most useful dahlias for me are the medium-sized cactus or decorative varieties with neat flowers on long straight stems, preferably in white, cream, pink, red, and soft lilac. Some are two-toned; some single-flowered. I wouldn't want to be without them.

The unfashionable carnation has been around for a very long time, cultivated for at least two thousand years. The flower-patterned background of the famous unicorn tapestries at New York's Cloisters Museum are rich in the flowers of medieval times: asphodel, columbine, lilies of the valley, cyclamen, and what medieval folk called "gilli flowers" and we call carnations. I love the small garden varieties known as "pinks," which have a unique scent of clove that makes them especially appealing to cut for the house. Unappreciated features of the commercial florists' carnation, however, are its glorious variety of color, long-lasting qualities, inexpensive price, and year-round availability.

A perennial garden is a good source for flowers. Shown are tall-growing hollyhocks, candelabra Verbascum bombyciferum "Polar Summer."

The red, pink, and white florists' carnations have landed on almost every street corner and unfortunately limit our perception of this versatile flower. But wonderful other colors are grown on the Italian Riviera and exported world-wide—lemon, apricot, soft lavender, and others with striped, bicolored petals that expand our flower vocabulary. I often combine fragrant, long-lasting carnations in garden bouquets of mixed flowers. The multiflowered spray carnations that are more delicate, versatile, and long-lasting are a "best buy" when garden flowers are in short supply. There are times and settings in which a large bouquet of carnations, perhaps in subtly shaded tones of white, cream, and lemon, can be stunningly effective when combined with the foliage of variegated hosta leaves, sprays of winter honeysuckle, or mock orange branches from the shrub border.

Harvesting from Nature

Over the garden wall, back in the woods that surround my home, I find nature—wild and uncultivated—to be a generous source of raw materials. Branches of blueberry, sapling birch, wild mountain laurel, rhododendron, and long trails of hardy English ivy are always at hand for my arrangements, plus pads of green moss, long ropes of wild grape, and the occasional bracket fungus. Some wild plants—Oriental bittersweet (*Celastus scandens*) and wild grape, for example—can grow rampantly to overwhelm the flowering dogwood or native cedar, particularly here on Long Island, and I have no hesitation in cutting them to twist into wreaths or baskets. But I always discourage haphazard cutting from nature. We must prune judiciously. When we stop the car to wrench off branches of flowering dogwood along the parkways, that is vandalism and a criminal act. A wise and responsible flower arranger will be familiar with the many choice plants on the endangered list that are not to be cut. The *Ilex verticillata*, or winterberry, the lycopodium, the ground pine or prince's-pine,

Cut flowers early in the morning if possible, while the dew is still on the grass.

our hardy "terrestial" orchids, such as the pink lady's slipper, should be admired and left to grow in peace. Picking anything in nature requires a healthy sense of civic responsibility to leave intact the growing things that will maintain each environment as nature intended and, equally important, give joy to those who pass by after we have left.

Buying Flowers

Florists, plant nurseries, and botanical gardens are also important sources of flowers and plants. The best of these are the farm stands where the flowers are fresh from the fields and the longest lasting once you get them home. Prices are usually reasonable since no middlemen or transportation costs are involved.

Nurseries and garden centers are the best sources of potted plants for around the patio or pool, or to brighten the front door. They are cheerful places to visit during the winter when we need an orchid, cyclamen, amaryllis, or maybe a spectacular bromeliad to perk up the house. It's a

very good idea for a regular flower customer to make friends with the owners of nurseries who may grow special materials or even start seeds for you. If you are on good terms with "Ernie" or "Sue," you'll know what's new, what's expected, and what will last the longest. Nursery staffs are great resources of gardening information and all sorts of helpful suggestions. The same is true of the personnel at retail florists. Once the manager and staff understand that you know and love flowers—and buy on a regular basis—they'll make special offers for you. More importantly, they'll give an honest answer about the origin or freshness of the stock and will stand by their product.

Botanical gardens and arboretums can be a bonanza for resources and ideas. I encourage anyone who lives within reach of a botanical garden to become a member. We can learn a lot in a hurry from experts in all fields of horticulture and get closer to those exotic flowers and plants. Very often, classes are given in growing plants or arranging flowers, and you can pick up the basics of botany and the history of your favorite flowers, plants, and even foods. Botanical gardens also sponsor field trips to parks, flower shows, and country research stations. Their libraries and book shops are well stocked in every horticultural topic. And don't overlook one of the major benefits from being a member of a local botanical garden: making friends with other flower lovers.

Botanical gardens and arboretums provide hands-on experience for people who do not have space or time for a garden of their own. They often rely on the volunteer efforts of their members. Learning to weed or prune in the gardens is a quick way to get to know different flowers and become actively involved with them. Even if you only offer to fill in behind the information desk on weekends, you will be in an environment where flowers are taken seriously and where you will be surrounded by like-minded folk. I am always amazed and delighted how a love of flowers breaks down shyness and creates instant friendship between strangers.

TOOLS
OF
THE
TRADE

LEFT: An old-fashioned container, like this cornucopia found at a junk shop, is the perfect container for an old-fashioned arrangement of mixed specie roses, clematis seed pods, hydrangea, and Korean chrysanthemums.

OPPOSITE: Baskets, pitchers, ceramic crocks, glass jars, cruets, vases, and metal containers—from the precious to the plebeian—can all be used to display flowers. A container needn't be "designed" for flowers—be creative!

PRECEDING PAGES:
Photograph by Horst.

LIVING WITH FLOWERS REQUIRES only a modest assortment of tools and equipment. Most important are the containers to hold the flowers themselves. Selecting the appropriate container for an arrangement of flowers is rather like selecting the right frame for a special painting. Like the frame, the container will become an integral part of the total effect. The flowers of the changing seasons or the setting in the house usually determine the pot for the job. For example, a fragrant gathering of first violets and grape hyacinths look great in an antique shaving mug. Daffodils bloom in such abundance that I fill glass water pitchers with them, all mixed and sweetly fragrant, for the dining table and guest rooms. However, with first blooms of a new variety—a pink trumpet, for example—I'll find a slender bottle and isolate them on the windowsill for special attention. When the peonies start to bloom, a tall blue and white ginger jar is the right "vase" for the moment. When early summer offers a wide assortment of flowers and weekend guests are coming, I make a large mixed bouquet in the Flemish style, by using a rather beaten but venerable old Sheffield plate tea urn, an old friend I know I can rely on to be the most accommodating container.

If you take the business of arranging flowers seriously, as I do, you will want to gather a variety of containers in a particular place, ready and waiting, where you can see them all at a quick glance. I suggest a cupboard, an unused wardrobe, or a spot under the stairs fixed up with shelves, a

fresh coat of paint, and perhaps a light. Your own style of living and particular tastes will determine your collection, but from my experience a variety of materials—pottery, glass, metal, wood, baskets, terra-cotta (with plenty of plastic liners)—allows for the greatest self-expression. Collecting containers will renew your interest in the tantalizing antique signs on back-country roads or the vegetable dish or earthenware casserole that has lost its lid and that you spotted at the neighbor's yard sale. A slightly chipped or broken handle needn't deter you, since household vessels in all sorts of condition are suitable if you are fond of them. The primary condition is that they be stable and capable of holding water.

For glass containers I constantly use flasks, bottles, and decanters, clear and colored, that hold one or two flowers to perfection. A large glass salad bowl is ideal for a collection of summer flowers, perhaps hydrangea, phlox, and lilies. And various styles and shapes of pitchers hold simply arranged flowers better than anything. I especially treasure a group of clear early American glass vases. These large-stemmed goblets come in a variety of sizes that dignify any group of flowers, and I often wonder why a modern version hasn't appeared. They combine elegance and simplicity in a direct and practical way.

I find the round, clear glass fishbowl to be one of the most basic and useful containers for many flowers. No mechanics are even needed. Keep the water level up to within an inch of the top, and the stems, held by the narrow opening, become part of the design. The arrangement is neither sophisticated nor contrived. Nothing is hidden, and the eye can appreciate the flower: stem, leaf, and blossom. If you are just starting out and can buy only one glass container, a fishbowl would be my suggestion.

When flowers are arranged in a glass bowl, to keep the water and container clean—and the flowers happy—try placing the entire arrangement in the sink and flushing fresh water

A favorite container that's "flower-friendly" can be used throughout the seasons of the year. In spring it might hold hyacinths, butterfly delphiniums, and ivy berries.

through the container until all is clear again. You don't need to remove the flowers from the vase; simply hold them steady.

Glass must be kept clean for appearance as well as hygiene. I recommend washing in warm soapy water after each use. Stubborn stains can be eased off by rubbing well with a slice of lemon dipped in salt. If the flask or bottle is narrow-necked and beyond the reach of a brush, try swirling fine sand around with detergent. The swirling motion will clean all the interior surfaces. Substitute a gentler abrasive, such as rice grains with a little baking soda, if the crystal is fine or precious.

Ceramic or pottery containers make up the bulk of my practical "standbys" and range from tiny pitchers to heroic footbaths, from delicate porcelain to hearty stoneware. In general, I prefer and would recommend plain shapes and solid basic colors, but I love a challenge and keep my eyes open for something unusual—a large shell, a stoneware mustard pot, even a fancy Victorian chamber pot, which would be perfect for a country bouquet or a flowering hydrangea plant.

Metal containers, whether copper, bronze, tole, enamel, or polished brass, add a distinctive touch to your resources. The soft gleam of silver is the most flattering complement for roses. I keep an antique copper watering can polished and gleaming for peach tulips with branches of flowering cherry or the tousled heads of late summer mums. Also on hand are a small pewter jug, two bronze mugs, a silver vegetable dish, and a venerable Georgian tea urn with its spout and inner workings removed. Once polished, metal containers can be clear lacquered to retain their shine, but I prefer to buff them with a little polish and a soft cloth from time to time. To cut down on polishing chores, I keep good silver things wrapped in soft cloth inside a polythene bag. As with glass bowls, metal containers should be cleaned after each use: remove chicken wire, needle holders, or other mechanics and give them a good scrub with a little disinfectant.

Baskets are right at home in any setting, since their many shapes, sizes, and finishes make them versatile and attractive. Your selection might include American Indian weave, Chinese bamboo, Japanese tea ceremony treasures, or rough, woven root and twig designs. Baskets are indispensable, especially for gift arrangements such as a low-growing spring garden of primroses, scilla, ivy in moss, or a mass of full garden roses. Any basket can be turned into a flower container with a waterproof liner, such as a plastic freezer container or deli tub.

Terra-cotta containers add a warm, reassuring, earthy look to an arrangement, whether they are antique flower pots, Mexican urns, or colonial redware. Because they are often low-fired and unglazed, they will be too porous to hold water and will also need a liner, such as a plastic freezer container. If the interior glaze seems inadequate, you can briefly heat the pot in a warm oven and pour in melted paraffin wax, swirling it around so that it comes into contact with all of the interior surfaces. Any small faults in the glaze will readily absorb the wax, and when it has cooled, the container should be able to hold water. I recommend a saucer or waterproof pad as insulation under earthenware containers that might "weep," and under metal containers where condensation might cause moisture.

Variety is the key word in choosing containers. Use your imagination to find the most appropriate ones, whether sleek and minimal as a simple glass column or funky and unlikely as a painted cookie jar.

Making Flowers Behave

In general, the most natural-looking arrangements are achieved by what the mother of a great flower-loving friend, the English painter and author Valentine Lawford, described as the "wodge and pronkle" method. As she explained to her son, there was no mystery in the business of arranging flowers. "You simply wodge them in the vase and pronkle them a little." Anyone who has ever put a handful of garden flowers in a vase understands exactly what these archaic English words mean. I call this technique the "into-the-vase plunge school" of flower arranging, and in many cases its disarming simplicity gets to the heart of the matter. Simply gather a generous grouping of flowers in the hand, trim the stems, set

In summer, the same container might be used for an arrangement of fragrant roses, hydrangea, and "love-in-a-mist."

ABOVE: This antique Chinese trough is a versatile container. It might hold plants or an arrangement, and could be used as a forcing container. The container can hold an arrangement like this one in which a large bracket fungus serves as a base. Sprays of roses, wild parsnip flowers, and ornamental grass complete the effect.

OPPOSITE: This fiberglass version of an Italian garden sculpture is good for the display of big flowers like the Sedum "Autumn Joy" and Fresca lilies with leaves of hosta.

Watering cans, like this battered veteran, are wonderful to keep around for quick arrangements. A Flemish mood is evoked with these exquisite Rembrandt tulips, dwarf lilacs, tree peonies, dwarf rhododendrons, and flowering herbs.

them into your favorite mug, jug, or vase, and let them spread out naturally. Tweak them a little, ease them apart with a few pokes, and you will have "pronkled" them into a pleasing arrangement. Flowers have a mind of their own and seem to arrange themselves with just a little nudging. Think of tulips, road weeds, or nasturtiums, and you'll know what I mean.

I would use this method for a handful of blue nigella (or more poetically, love-in-a-mist), nepeta, or cat mint with some tall sprigs of forget-me-not combined sweetly in a striped pitcher. I pick cosmos by the jugful, stripping stems as I gather them on an evening stroll. Another bunch, with Queen Anne's lace, bladder champion, bouncing bet, or streamers of wild honeysuckle will all go into an ancient apothecary jar with absolutely no fuss. Besides, in summer the simple flowers will not last very long anyway and should be picked and enjoyed instantly.

Chicken wire is one of the handiest aids for arranging flowers when the "wodge and pronkle" method is too haphazard and you are working for a more formal effect. When using a large bowl or a wide-mouthed jug, for example, I insert two or three thicknesses of chicken wire, gently folded

and crumpled into a ball to fill the vessel loosely. It should press against the sides of the container and be held firmly in place with strips of narrow florist tape secured around the lip of the vessel. You can now easily insert the flowers through the wire so that they are held at the angle you prefer them. Use the heavier branching materials first to create a silhouette or outline of the entire arrangement. Their stems will establish a supporting web for the lighter flowers as they are added. Finally, insert the most delicate flowers and the feature or focal group that unites the composition. When I am using a glass vase and don't want the chicken wire to show, I fit a double layer of wire cut to fit as a lid across the mouth of the vase or jug and hold it rigidly in place with adhesive floral tape. Remember that whenever you work with tape, the vessel, the wire, and your hands must be completely dry or the tape will not stick.

The needlepoint or pin holder used by many arrangers is an import from Japan where it is called a *kenzan*. It is made of a heavy lead base with steel or brass pins protruding up from it. Pin holders come in various shapes: circular, square, oblong, and half-moon. They are used extensively by the Japanese in the art of flower arranging known as ikebana. One modern style, called moribana, is usually presented in a low bowl or tray and offers a stylized landscape display that on closer inspection proves to be skillfully contrived, following very specific principles of design. The pin holder is indispensable for these arrangements, assuring absolute control of each flower and stalk. I appreciate and greatly admire the Japanese art of flower arrangement, which can remind us of the great beauty of simplicity and restraint, where less is more.

By using a pin holder as an anchor I can arch a spray of early camellia over water in a shallow pewter bowl with a few stones, or create the effect of a tall bearded iris rising simply amid its own foliage from a heavy glass bowl. Without a doubt, a variety of these holders increases the design possibilities. I often place a heavy pin holder below crumpled chicken wire at the bottom of a big vase to firmly anchor the tallest, heaviest stems of flowering crab apple or magnolia in a mixed arrangement of long-stemmed spring flowers. With a large pin holder and some chicken wire I can provide stability and weight in a large baking dish or bowl filled with a mass of lilacs, early roses, or peonies. As with all tools and equipment, pin holders should be kept clean and scrubbed occasionally with a strong brush to remove bits of oasis or stem fragments. A soak in bleach is also a good periodic treatment. It's good housekeeping and best done as you empty containers after each use.

Probably the greatest aid to flower arranging has been the invention of oasis, or floral foam, a firm, green, water-absorbing substance made from plastic foam granules that are compressed into block form. Oasis can be cut into any desired shape to fit specific vases. It weighs practically nothing but absorbs and retains an amazing amount of water. There are two grades available: instant oasis, which is less dense and recommended for finer or soft-stemmed flowers, such as tulip and other garden flowers; and standard oasis,

which is heavier and can support even woody branches in larger arrangements. Each stem should have an angled cut and be inserted into the block of oasis at whatever position or angle is needed for the design.

With oasis, flowers can appear to defy the law of gravity when arranged, as if they are falling and in tumbling over the edge of an urn or included in a lush flowered garland that spirals up a column. I can also develop extra height for a tall arrangement by building up a cone of oasis secured within chicken wire, thus creating the effect of very long-stemmed flowers and foliage for a large display.

Oasis provides both a source of water for cut flowers and the means to hold them in place. We can even dispense with a container of water altogether if need be and work on a shallow tray. Simply submerge oasis in water, and when all the air bubbles cease, it is completely saturated and ready for use. Because oasis so efficiently absorbs and holds a large amount of water, most flowers will last in it for considerable periods of time, even several days if necessary. Foliage of all kinds—ivy and woody-stemmed evergreens, such as cedar, pieris, azalea, rhododendron, or palm fronds—are happy in oasis pads wrapped in plastic and tied to tent poles, for example, where they will stay fresh for an evening garden party. For short-term occasions, oasis allows you to be much more imaginative and frees you from the limitations of standard containers.

For the weekend house in the country, you could put together an arrangement that looks like freshly cut flowers lying in the gathering basket just as they were picked. They only seem to be waiting to be arranged, for in fact the stem ends are firmly in place and well watered by a hidden block of oasis in a low plastic liner or bowl amply covered with leaves and the large full blooms of rose or peony. Oasis is also perfect for transporting gifts of cut flowers. You can arrange them from the garden without the worry of water spilling on the journey, and you know they'll still be perfect when you arrive.

No container? No problem. A hollowed-out watermelon can be filled with roses and baby's breath. Any kind of melon will do, as will pumpkins, squash, or eggplant.

HOW TO
USE AN
OASIS RING

Oasis rings can be a real boon for flower arrangers. The choice of sizes available make them very adaptable. You can surround a narrow candlestick or a large hurricane shade. All you need to do is soak the ring (perhaps add a little flower preservative to the water first) and begin arranging the flowers. Use care when inserting the stems, which should be cut on a sharp angle. "Base" the ring first with short ivy trails, galax leaves, or low spurs of flowering crab apple or viburnum. Then complete the design with a few full, short-stemmed blossoms. A cluster of small lady apples impaled on a pick among greens, roses, or holly berries makes a great winter or Christmas display. Knowing how easy it is to use an oasis ring will free your imagination to come up with endless ideas. I recommend you set the oasis ring on a plate or shallow tray (such as a pizza pan) that will hold a small reservoir of water so as not to damage a table or tablecloth. If care is taken when inserting and removing the flowers, you can get two or three uses from each oasis ring. Simply store the ring, kept damp in a sealed plastic bag, until you are ready to use it again for your next party.

154

There are several problems to watch for with oasis, however. The stems of some flowers may absorb particles of oasis, which can clog the cellular tissue and result in premature wilting. Tulips and roses may actually lose water by a process of "reverse absorption" if the block of oasis is not fully soaked. Because oasis has such powerful absorbing properties, as it becomes dry, it can suck moisture from the flower stems themselves with devastating results. Therefore, one final suggestion: when using floral foam to support flowers, keep the vase topped with water because the entire surface of oasis allows water to evaporate, and the water level can drop more quickly than you might imagine. Also, when soaking oasis blocks, dissolve some flower food, such as Plant Life or Floralife, in the water, to give flowers that little extra encouragement.

Years ago I used oasis in a centerpiece for a friend's evening dinner party. I was astounded when, a year later, she

BELOW: A couple of roses with some Champagne grapes might just be the quick dress-up you're looking for when throwing a party or when unexpected guests are on the way.

OPPOSITE: A range of outdoor topiaries and flowering plants in tubs (to be brought inside when needed) can be used throughout the summer, even year-round with proper care.

told me that the arrangement was "still growing." Of course, the cut flowers had long since died and been removed, but some of the exotic foliage I used had taken root in the oasis and was still thriving. So even though it is made of plastic, oasis is not a totally unsympathetic medium for living things.

Moss and pebbles can provide a very natural-looking base for certain flower arrangements. As an anchoring technique, marbles and polished stones can look attractive in a clear glass vase. Besides adding an aesthetic dimension, they will hide a pin holder. Moss can create a wonderful landscape or garden effect in low arrangements and also camouflage mechanical techniques. Both sheet moss and bun moss are lifted from the ground in flat pads. Sheet moss, which is available commercially, will keep indefinitely if stored dry and soaked when needed. Bun moss I gather in my woods at the base of trees and among the leaves. Spanish moss, available from Florida and very popular, is not a true moss but a bromeliad, which will stay alive if kept moist; it lends a haunting touch of gray to an arrangement while hiding the wire, oasis, or other mechanical aids.

Lastly, the useful rubber-capped water piks provide compact reservoirs for individual flowers. Although they belong in the professional's "tricks of the trade," the amateur arranger or hobbyist can borrow this technique to great advantage. The hidden tube of water, attached to a slender cane or branch, will let you position flowers in arrangements independently of the containers. For example, water piks are extremely handy in such demanding situations as a summer wedding, where fresh flowers are to be grouped in a swag over a chapel doorway and fastened with ribbon to the church pews.

The Essential Tools

Not having the proper equipment and tools need not deter you from improvising on the spot. After all, one doesn't usually take along oasis, chicken wire, and pin holders on weekend outings to the country, on vacations, or when visiting friends. When we need flowers in our lives, and they are waiting to be arranged, we may not be able to run out and buy all the necessary tools. Often nature can provide the solution. For example, three or four inches of sand in the bottom of a vase will anchor most flowers in lieu of a pin holder or oasis. Cut branches of evergreen or a handful of birch twigs twisted and wedged into an old bedroom jug can provide a short-term

This Capodimonte urn, a junk-store find, presents flowers very well. Its height allows for arrangements where vines and flowers can trail down.

webbing almost as reliable as crumpled chicken wire and much more attractive. For a low casserole container, stretch aluminum foil over the top, secure it with string, and puncture small holes in it. Insert short-stemmed flowers through the openings and hide the foil with foliage or moss.

If you are planning to acquire tools or add the basics you need for flower arranging, here are a few fundamentals every flower arranger should have on hand:

- A pair of heavy-duty loppers or pruners to cut woody branches and flowering shrubs

- A pair of secateurs or pruning shears (I recommend the Felco or Wilkinson brands.)

- A pair of sharp scissors (indispensable)

- A sharp paring or Swiss Army–type knife for scraping stems and making fresh cuts

- A retired kitchen knife to cut oasis

- A reel of lightweight green florist's wire for many chores: to hold a plastic liner in a basket, to wire a basket to a veranda post, to secure a narrow basket on a mantle

- Small bundle of annealed wire (usually green in color) in twelve- or eighteen-inch lengths of grades 20, 22, and 26, to strengthen or straighten a stem or to wrap around a bunch of small-stemmed flowers

- Rubber bands for bunching tiny flowers together as you cut them in the garden or gather them in the wild, especially violets, nasturtium, or cornflowers

- Modeling clay to anchor a pin holder to a dish, secure a loose candle, or even keep a piece of fruit stable on a tray

- Newspaper, great for packing flowers before travel, wrapping weak-stemmed flowers before conditioning, and as a layer to stop a pin holder from sliding over the bottom of a ceramic bowl

- A few narrow bamboo canes to stiffen or splint a weak stem of a tall lily or delphinium

- A durable plastic pump "mister" for spraying flowers and plants

- A wooden mallet and board for crushing stems

- Flower food to be added to water

- Household bleach for cleanups and to help keep water fresh in a large bowl of mixed flowers

Perfecting Your Technique

Whenever I lecture and demonstrate the simple and pleasurable joys of flower arranging, I hear the comment, "You make it look so easy." And so it is, I explain, when you express your ideas with flowers in the most direct and best manner possible—and as quickly as possible too. Flowers are living things and should be handled firmly, gently, and as little as necessary. Choose the appropriate container for the flowers and the setting, use whatever mechanical aids are necessary, and have confidence that creativity and your innate good taste will win the day.

Of course there are general guidelines for flower arrangements, just as there are for any artistic composition, including scale, form, proportion, and balance. Take balance,

The utility of old watering cans as containers cannot be overstated. A new one will do, but they seem nicest when slightly used.

for example, which is critical in most arrangements. If the finished display looks top-heavy for the container or table, or veers wildly to one side, it will have a disturbing effect, but much worse, it might be physically off balance and come crashing down during the party.

How does one go about learning all this? As with cooking, swimming, or playing golf, we learn flower arranging by practice. No matter what family or friends say, trust the fact that you know and love flowers, and start modestly with a simple bunch or a single peony; then begin to add, growing bigger and bolder as you progress.

I suggest observing flowers and foliage in the garden and in the wild and let their natural patterns of growth and movement inspire your arranging. In other words, arrange flowers as they grow. Delphinium, foxglove, and ornamental grasses stand tall and so I use them for their height. Ivy, honeysuckle, jasmine, climbing roses, and wisteria reach out and hang down and so I position them for a "tumbling out" effect. The wide arching branches of flowering crab apple or buddleia are perfect to establish the width of a design, while the round shapes of hydrangea, full peony, and clusters of phlox provide the bulk and beauty to fill in and complete the large mass arrangement that is the summer garden incarnate.

In a mixed collection of flowers and foliage, I tend to work with and arrange one type of material at a time. For example, after the chicken wire, oasis, or pin holder is securely in place, I will usually start with heavier, lower branches that lie against the rim of the bowl and reach out to the sides to establish the width of the arrangement. With these I create the basic architecture of the display and the relationship it will have with the container. Next I insert the tallest flowers to establish the height of the design, and then proceed to fill in with shorter bulky forms, again working with one type of flower at a time and with regard for the colors involved, positioning the strongest colors or boldest forms for maximum effect.

Experience builds confidence, and after a time, the spontaneous, logical sequence comes naturally: heavy or bulky materials first, then the lighter, more delicate flowers. If you begin with an idea in mind that takes into account the container, the occasion, and the setting, and work from this preconceived plan, you know more or less where you are going as you work. Of course, flower arranging is not a construction job that requires a blueprint. Rather it is an organic process that proceeds and develops according to the unique combination of materials you are using. Keep an open mind, be a little daring, stand back and take a long look as you proceed, and enjoy the experiment as you go along.

ABOVE: Terra-cotta containers with glazed interiors are handsome vessels for flowers and plants. If you're wary of a container's ability to hold moisture, line it. A hybrid gloxinia thrives here.

OPPOSITE: Scissors are the do-everything tool for arrangers. These Chinese scissors are recommended. The antique porcelain gravy boat holds a collection of David Austin's roses, including pink Heirloom, creamy Proud Titania, rosy Lucetta, and red Fisherman's Friend varieties.

CARE
AND
CONDITIONING

HAVING SPENT MUCH OF MY LIFE in the "flower business" I have observed that there are many ways to make flowers last longer and be coaxed into giving an extended performance. There is no alchemy or secret magic for keeping flowers fresh—just a few basic pointers that can make all the difference in the world. In most cases there are no special steps other than gathering and quickly getting the flowers into fresh, clean water. Fleshy-stemmed flowers, like many lilies, tulips, or daffodils and popular annuals like cosmos, snaps, or nasturtiums, will do nicely with just this simple care. Woody-stemmed flowers, such as Queen Anne's lace, hydrangea, and lilac, however, require a little more attention, but the basics are very simple.

In the Garden

First, let's make sure we head off into the garden properly prepared. I always take a basket, pruning shears, and a sharp knife or scissors, as well as a supply of rubber bands; in hot weather, I'll probably put buckets of water in the wheelbarrow. The best time to go out gathering is either early in the morning with the dew on the flowers or in the cool of the evening after the sun has gone down; then the sap has risen and the flowers will be quite firm. If you pick flowers in the heat of the day, you may find they rapidly collapse; so, if you can, it's better to take them while they are firm and in prime condition. I prefer to cut flowers and foliage in the evening rather than the morning because then I can leave them in water overnight to condition and they will be ready for action in the morning.

As I cut, I bunch similar flowers together according to stem length, clustering together the smaller flowers, like nasturtiums or sweet peas with a rubber band, keeping longer-stemmed flowers like cornflowers and zinnias in bunches of their own. This makes handling them much easier and prevents them from getting damaged as they might if they were just put loosely into the basket. With long-stemmed flowers, such as cleome or Italian sunflowers, I can let their heads hang over the edge of the basket so they won't get crushed. A basket with a long, low tray, or what is known in England as a trug, is ideal for this. If I am out gathering on a hot day or there is no cloud cover, I definitely recommend putting the flowers, especially roses, immediately into buckets of water so they will not collapse on the way back to the house.

If you have a garden, and the time, it is the ultimate pleasure to grow your own flowers. Plan a cutting garden in the winter and enjoy your summer favorites fresh and available on demand. Add a few rows of the flowers you really enjoy—like cosmos, lisianthus, hybrid lilies, snapdragons, or nigellas—to the vegetable garden or maybe along the side of the house or garage, even at the edge of the yard or woods. Planting not so much for show as for cutting, you can grow what you like to use for arrangements and special occasions during the summer and fall months, such as dahlias.

Just as dedicated bird lovers are never without a pair of binoculars nearby, we who love flowers are always prepared for spontaneous foraging trips. I keep a basket, a pair of shears, and some newspaper in the station wagon at all times. Then if one of nature's treasures catches my eye along the roadside, and all is clear, I can pull over, cut it, and take it with me. When I am out on the lecture circuit, it can be an adventure setting out with pruners, a large drop cloth, damp newspaper, string, and gloves, to roam the edge of a river or the spring woods looking for budding branches or long-stemmed flowers that I can use in demonstration. Nature never seems to fail but offers some branches of chestnut or stalks of teasel that are just waiting to be discovered and taken back to share with a surprised audience.

Intelligent foraging is required, however. Certain invasive exotics like bittersweet (*Celastrus*), the rose hips of *Rosa foliosa*, grasses, and runaway ivy are worth seeking out, but natives on conservation lists such as scarlet winterberry or flaming butterfly weed and native dogwood are to be respected. Observe "No Trespassing" notices and be sensitive and courteous when invited to cut from a friend's garden. Choose branches from the lower level or the back of a shrub and don't cut all the flowers you need from any one area, and be careful where you tread.

ABOVE: These America, Cherish, and Butterscotch climbing roses and "love-in-a-mist" can be cut throughout the season. Grown together, they can be arranged together for a natural look.

Cutting the Flowers

A basic rule for gathering is to cut stems as long as possible because you can always shorten them but never graft back on. It helps to have in mind how you are going to employ the flowers you gather so that you can pick to suit certain vases, containers, or a specific setting. Always make a clean cut with sharp secateurs, scissors, or a knife and gather stems of differing lengths that include some contrasting buds among the mature flowers. When picking spring-flowering bulbs, I leave as much foliage as possible as this is the food factory that feeds the plant for the coming year. With bulbs such as daffodils, hyacinths, or tulips, you can usually simply pull the flowers. Grasp the stem well down, give a sharp tug, and it will snap easily and not harm the bulb. Among the reliable summer crop, dahlias, zinnias, and cosmos, for example, these continue to make new growth and bloom vigorously through the growing season the more the flowers are kept cut; so as I move through the garden, I deadhead the sweet peas or cut off spent roses to encourage the new blooms.

Roses, in particular, require clean cuts with sharp tools because the bushes are susceptible to disease. A precise diagonal cut above a new bud or node will encourage new growth. Continual deadheading of old blooms and trimming of canes is vital, along with feeding and spraying against mildew or blackspot.

Experience is the best teacher for learning at which stage to cut flowers. Generally speaking, the advanced bud stage is best, when the outer or lower blossoms are mature and well colored. Most spring bulbs open readily from a mature bud and, in fact, much of the enjoyment of these most-welcome flowers comes from watching their development in water. (Tulips, for example, continue to expand and "grow" in interesting ways after cutting.) Violets require full maturation, however, because their buds don't open readily in water. Lilies should have at least the first flowers open, while lilacs and hydrangeas should be almost fully open before cutting. Pick all poppies in extended bud and watch their fragile sepals dry and split open to reveal the silken ruffles.

Zinnia, stock, delphinium, peony, aster, and most garden flowers are best gathered as they approach maturity, when the bloom is almost fully open and the color well developed. The same holds true for tropical flowers such as strelitzia, ginger, and other near exotics like agapanthus, galtonia, and pineapple lilies. Pinch out the extreme tip of a spike of gladiolus or the terminal buds of a spray of tuberose; it stops growth and encourages the lower flowers to open.

Conditioning Freshly Cut Flowers

Every flower arranger needs a special work space, perhaps a corner of the laundry area, or deserves at least a bench in the garage or side porch, if not a place in the kitchen. Half the fun of working with flowers is knowing that you can bang, scrape, get dirty if necessary, and even let a little soil fall on the floor. Convenience is important for doing your best and getting the most pleasure from your work, so keep tools, materials, and containers handy and try to set up your work area near a sink since you will need hot and cold running water. If you are limited to the confines of a tiny kitchen or arranging flowers in situ, such as in a church or a living room, I recommend a drop cloth to keep your "mess" within bounds.

Treatment of flowers is as varied as the wonderful varieties of flowers themselves, but following are some basic rules for conditioning.

Remove all the foliage that will be beneath the water level to reduce bacterial growth and keep the water cleaner longer, a must for getting the best performance out of a bouquet. A teaspoon of household bleach will keep everything fresh and clear if you have arranged the flowers in a glass vase and especially with woody-stemmed plants or shrubs, which can quickly discolor the water.

For soft-stemmed flowers, such as nasturtiums, marigolds, sweet peas, forget-me-nots, and spring flowers as noted, remove any leaves that will be below the water line and make a clean cut, then arrange them in cool fresh water.

For woody-stemmed flowers, including garden chrysanthemums, stock, and perennial aster, as well as such flowering shrubs as mock orange, lilac, and magnolia, there are techniques I describe as *scraping*, *bruising*, and *boiling*—one of these will do the job and you need to experiment. Pay attention, class!

SCRAPING: With woody stems of forsythia, shrub roses, and magnolia, scrape the bark off the lower three inches of the stem with a sharp pocket knife, then make a clean diagonal cut with your pruner and another cut

ABOVE: Some flowers are prone to wilting and if their "bark" is scraped off, water will be able to get to the proper tissue better. Use this technique for roses and other flowering shrubs.

BELOW: Crushing or bruising the stems of woody-stemmed flowers, such as rhododendron, stock, chrysanthemum, and lilac, can also help with water absorption and prolong a flower's life. Use a mallet, hammer, or any blunt instrument.

up the stem before standing to condition in a tall container of warm water.

BRUISING: Also effective with woody stems of such flowers as garden chrysanthemums, stock, spirea, and viburnum, try bruising the bottom 3–4 inches of these stems with a wooden mallet or hammer. Remove all lower foliage or weak side shoots and don't pulverize the stems. A couple of sharp cracks will be sufficient to break up the tough tissue and encourage transpiration.

BOILING: A seemingly brutal treatment that does the trick with woody-stemmed flowers I know to be difficult, and here I include hydrangea, astilbe, and the "summer weeds" we all love: Queen Anne's lace, joe-pye weed, black-eyed Susan, as well as the hollow-stemmed hollyhock, delphinium, and even dahlia. Prepare the flowers first; remove all lower leaves and keep stem ends together before plunging them into 3–4 inches of very hot water for 30–60 seconds. Immediately transfer to a container of cold or lukewarm water to condition them in a cool place.

Lilac is one tricky shrub that needs particular care. Firstly pick sprays where at least half of the flowers are already open, remove all or almost all of the foliage, and bruise the stems before giving the boiling water treatment for about 60 seconds, and then allow to settle in a container of cool water in a cool shady spot.

Now we come to *burning*: With flowers that exude a milky sap—all members of the euphorbia family, such as poinsettia, as well as the poppy clan and oleander—remove lower foliage and hold the stem ends over a candle or gas burner for 15–20 seconds, this carbonizes the latex liquid that would otherwise block the water conducting cells. Then condition as usual in lukewarm water before arranging.

Roses may be considered separately, but some of the above treatments are useful: with blooms from the garden, I remove thorns and lower leaves, and then suggest scraping the stem ends with a sharp knife and recutting the stems before arranging in lukewarm water. With long-stemmed roses from the florist, it may be a good idea to strip off many of the leaves and remove any crushed petals, shorten the stems by a half, make a clean diagonal cut with a sharp knife or pruners, and arrange in warm water in a clean container. I would also suggest you recut the stems and change the water in a day or two. And don't forget that a dash of bleach will keep the water clear.

Plants and flowers take up warm water more readily than cold. Use water at room temperature rather than icy tap water in the vase. However, the benefit of lower temperatures is well demonstrated by the ability to keep plants and flowers for prolonged periods in cool storage. For example, peonies wrapped dry can be kept in arrested development for three to four weeks. Hyacinth and daffodil plants can also be kept on hold for extended periods. Cold slows down the whole growth and metabolic rate; thus it is no mystery that cut flowers will last considerably longer when kept cool, especially during the night.

Reviving Flowers

It seems inevitable that some flowers will start to wilt or fade in an arrangement before others. Like humans, some flowers are robust and hardy, while others have less energy and quickly grow dispirited. But over the years I have learned that wilted doesn't mean wasted. Rather than throw out a fading flower, I use several easy techniques that produce what I call the "Lazarus effect."

One of these techniques is a simple bath. Remove a tired flower from the arrangement, strip off as much foliage as practical, and make a clean cut and split the stem. Then lay the whole thing in shallow water in the bathtub or large wash tub for a half hour or so. Since every part of the flower—stem, leaf, and blossom—absorbs water, soaking them in this way allows the flower to drink up as much water as possible. Such a bath can be amazingly restorative and will often perk up sadly drooping flowers and extend their lives. Following this, I would recommend the hot water technique—especially with hydrangea or lilac—to complete the reconditioning treatment.

Sometimes I confess I have to resort to more rigorous measures. I may use a slender bamboo cane inside the hollow stem of a heavy amaryllis or a piece of florist wire as a splint to support the weak stem of a hothouse rose or gerbera. One device I frequently employ is a toothpick inserted through the center of a zinnia to prevent its head from snapping over. This trick really works, especially when flowers are in short supply and all of your blooms are important.

Flowers that have traveled long distances from the country house, the farm stand, or the market may need special "welcome home" care. Soft tulips, gerberas, and peonies can be helped by recutting the stems and rolling them loosely in a tube of newspaper and placing them upright in buckets of water in a cool place for an hour or two. Capillary action draws the water up the newspaper and rapidly helps to stiffen the stem, foliage, and flowers.

Wilting and reviving are part of the natural cycle of a flower's daily life. In the heat of a summer's day, flowers tend to droop a bit, but they always revive quickly in the cooler air of the evening. You can work with this natural process by letting flowers that are to travel wilt a bit on a journey and then revive them by one of the techniques I've described. You may enjoy, as I do, watching people's amazed reactions to just how well these "Lazarus techniques" really work.

A basic rule for keeping cut flowers fresh is to make sure the water level is topped up. Flowers are remarkable pumping devices and through a process called transpiration they "drink" up lots of water, which eventually passes out through the petals and foliage. It is not really necessary to change the water each time you freshen up the flowers; just add fresh clean water to top off the vase, with a teaspoon of bleach to kill bacteria. It's especially important to monitor the water level with flowers that are arranged in oasis. Since the material itself is absorbent, water evaporates from its entire surface, causing the water level to drop surprisingly fast.

A Spoonful of Sugar

There are numerous "folk remedies" for making cut flowers last longer—everything from aspirins to copper pennies—and I constantly run into people who swear that they work. It leads me to wonder if there might not be a placebo effect among flowers and the added attention, in whatever form, gives them the will to live! Nonetheless, here are my comments on the various additives.

Aspirin may be beneficial. It contains salicylic acid, a substance derived from two natural sources. The acid retards bacterial development.

A few drops of chlorine creates a very mild hydrochloric acid, which works as above.

The addition of sugar to the vase makes sucrose available, which can be absorbed to help make up for the loss of natural plant juices. But too much can increase bacterial growth.

Vodka or other alcohol has the same effect as sugar.

A copper penny is of very questionable value, although in theory imperceptible amounts of copper could become soluble to create a copper sulphate or chloride, which would act as a fungicide or algicide.

Alum is useful with long-lasting flowers (mature hydrangea heads, for example) when water is hard. This causes precipitation of such chemicals as magnesium and calcium and therefore purifies the water.

Commercial products, such as Floralife, often contain a silver-based compound, silver nitrate, that has preservative abilities. Their use delays senescence—the plant growth phase from full maturity to death that is characterized by an accumulation of metabolic products and a loss in dry weight—especially in leaves and fruit. Growers and commercial flower shippers employ these chemicals to delay or control the opening of flowers shipped in bud,

ABOVE: When removing pollen, you may be prolonging the life of the flower. The waxy pollen is devastating to clothing and upholstery and should be removed when flowers are placed near people or furniture.

FOLLOWING PAGE: Only after the shortest day of the year can one force a branch of forstythia, quince, cherry, dogwood, or birch. In a bucket of water, create a mini-greenhouse for the branches with clear plastic sheets. Mist the branches occasionally. Allow three to four weeks for a generous display of blossoms.

such as carnations, chrysanthemums, tulips, and peonies. It is important not to use these products in metal containers, which can change the chemical makeup, but they are especially useful for summer flowers in simple vases and during conditioning.

Charcoal can also be a useful additive. Being an absorbent, it helps remove bad odors and undesirable coloring from the water of an arrangement of mixed greenery or one intended to last a long time.

The above ideas are no substitute for good hygiene. Scrub containers between uses in sudsy water with a dash of ammonia or bleach, and keep the water in the vases fresh.

Some Other "Lasting" Tips

When a flower has pollen that has ripened and dispersed, it has completed a part of its natural cycle and will begin to fade. With lilies, I always remove the conspicuous stamens as soon as the buds open. This delays the development of the flower, and prevents the waxy stain that can make a mess of clothing or upholstery if you even brush by the nodding stamens.

Perhaps you didn't know, but the presence of ethylene gas from a bowl of ripe apples, for example, can hasten the development of the flower and thus its deterioration. When flowers are improperly stored, the decaying process of petals and leaves can also release this oxidant. So, a fresh atmosphere is clearly best for the life of your cut flowers. However, the presence of the gas can also be helpful. A bromeliad can sometimes be induced to develop a flower spike by enclosing the plant within a large clear plastic bag along with a ripe apple. Maybe those tight rosebuds can be stimulated to open up with the same trick, but caution is advised.

High heat and low humidity in the house are unnatural conditions, and can shorten the flower's life faster than anything else. By simply placing an arrangement or flowering plant in a cool spot overnight you can greatly extend its

beauty and life. An unheated room, back porch, or mud room with night temperatures in the 40s or 50s is ideal; it allows the flowers to recuperate as they would outdoors. This is especially true here in the Northeast, where our houses in winter are so warm and dry. For the sake of my furniture, books, and a clear head, I keep a humidifier going from December through April and the flowers can appreciate the difference.

A Word About Vases

The most satisfactory containers for flower arranging are made of glass, glazed pottery, or nonferrous metal. However, baskets, wooden buckets, garden urns, and even terra-cotta pots cunningly fitted with plastic liners are all possible containers for your next creation. So save those deli containers!

I rely on softly crumpled chicken wire, either within the vessel or stretched across the top of a tall vase and secured with tape. You do not need a dense ball of wire, but rather a supporting web to hold the stems naturally as you proceed. The floral foam Oasis is the most popular aid, used alone or in combination with chicken wire, especially when flowers are being delivered to a party or I am creating a major opus involving large branches and a heroic display of flowers.

Forcing Branches in Winter

My guests and friends always smile when they see spring flowering branches that I have forced into early bloom for winter arrangements, and ask how this can be done without a greenhouse. Actually, anyone can make spring happen early by forcing branches, and some are easier than others. If you want to watch spring unfold in January or February, gather branches of dormant trees and shrubs that are early bloomers, such as forsythia, flowering quince, winter sweet, witch hazel, pussy willow, *Cornus mas* and winter cherry. Prune these anytime after the winter solstice as the days grow longer. I try to select interesting branches with sweep and line rather than just straight sticks, and cut or prune intelligently so as not to ruin the shape of the shrub or tree. Bring them inside, crush the stems, and stand them in an unheated room or garage in warm water and mist then twice a day, if possible. As the buds begin to show color, move them into the house in generous groups: the winter days will be brighter as you wait for spring to arrive indoors. I suggest you continue to cut a few branches each week to have a sequence of flowers. This slow development may take from three to six weeks but will give the best results: fatter buds, longer-lasting flowers, and more color as well, if the process takes place in a well-lit area.

For extra warmth and humidity, which are the secrets of forcing, one can create a greenhouse effect around the branches with a tent of clear plastic. (Use a dry-cleaning bag.) Forcing may sound like a brutal process, but it is really a very gentle one—one you will acquire easily with experience and patience. No reason to be without spring in January and February or March, as there are so many flowering bulbs that can brighten the windowsill when the snow is deep outside. Paper white narcissus are certainly the easiest to force, either on pebbles, in potting soil, or in a soilless mix, and once you have mastered these you can experiment with miniature daffodils, such as "tête-à-tête," and muscari, crocus, or the fragrant, reliable hyacinth. I get the best results when I keep the potted bulbs in a cool dark place (anywhere above freezing), in a cupboard, cellar, or garage for two to three weeks to stimulate root growth. The cooler the growing conditions, the more substantial and longer-lasting the flowers will be. Grow them on to bloom in the window of a back porch, a garage, or an attic with minimum heat—even the unheated spare bedroom.

Preserving Flowers

Drying and preserving flowers is a wonderful way to make them last months, sometimes years, and provide pleasure long beyond their natural life cycle. There are several ways to preserve flowers.

Some summer flowers, such as roses, hydrangea, and larkspur, can be dried naturally in a vase before the flower's color fades. Let the water dry up, rather than top it off. Here's a hint: try a little hairspray to keep the petals in place.

If you grow flowers specifically for drying, cut them in the morning after the dew dries and get them into an environment with warm, dry air, such as an attic, as soon as possible. Hang them upside down, firmly tied in tidy bunches where there is a current of dry air—and that's it! Some short-stemmed flowers can be placed on sheets of foil and dried in a kitchen oven on the lowest temperature setting with the door open. The more quickly flowers are dried, of course, the more natural they will appear.

If you have patience, try silica gel, a preferred medium for drying individual flowers. Other useful dehydrating agents can include combinations of borax, alum, sand, and kitty litter for different plant material. Fill a shoe box, a plastic storage container, or a deep tray or drawer with about one inch of the medium. Gently push the stem into the drying agent up to the head, and gently trickle the gel over and around each flower head to bury it. The flower will dry very quickly (within a week), will shrink slightly, and will lose little color, although your flower is now very brittle. Flowers that are easy to dry in this manner are roses, pansies, dahlias, and marigolds. Arranging your finished bouquet takes patience and skill: the flowers can either be wired or glued to artificial stems and placed into a bowl containing oasis or moss, or even sand. Flowers will dry naturally in silica gel in two to three days, in borax or alum in three to ten days. Note that certain flowers with heavy heads may best be wired before drying, such as dahlias and helichrysums.

In today's terms, drying flowers in a microwave oven is an "instant" method, and the color is well retained. Preheat the gel to insure it is completely dry, then lay one to two inches in an oven dish, set the flower heads, and gently cover with more gel. It only takes two to three minutes, depending on the flowers being dried, and a little experimenting will be necessary to perfect your technique. Be sure to set the container aside for half an hour before removing the flowers.

Branches of robust foliage from trees, such as southern magnolia, beech, or oak, and stems of berries, like wild rose hips, can be preserved with a glycerine solution and used in winter arrangements over and over again. Cut the branches late in the season when the leaves are quite mature. Scarlet or pin oak, for example, should be cut in the autumn when the color has developed. Wait several hours or overnight to allow the cut stems to wilt slightly; in this condition they will more eagerly drink up the preserving solution. Wash off or rinse the foliage in cold water and split the lower six inches of the stems in two or three places to encourage absorption. Next, place the branches into a solution of two parts hot or boiling water to one part glycerine. Make sure the stems are submerged at least six inches. Check the water level regularly. Leave the branches in a dim, dust-free room for about two to three weeks, at which time the foliage will have turned a rich golden brown or bronze. A little flower dye added to the glycerine solution can subtly change the finished effect. The use of a pleasant green, for example, may help to retain the summer effect of beech leaves, while a red dye could enhance the autumn colors of scarlet oak. Experimenting here is the key, but restraint please. Remember, you are only interested in creating a natural effect, not a bizarre one. It may be necessary to brush the extremities of the branches with the solution once a week if the mixture is not drawn up to the leaf tips. You'll know when your branches are ready: the leaves will still be supple with little beads of moisture appearing on them. At this point, I either use the entire branch with its foliage as it is, or remove branches with leaves and store them in dust-free boxes until I need them.

Pressing Flowers

Flowers from the summer border can easily be pressed by placing them between sheets of newspaper or paper towels and laying these between the pages of a large book, such as a dictionary or telephone directory, or under the corner of a carpet. Don't worry about the flower staining the pages of the book; the color will remain in the flower. In two to three weeks all moisture will be absorbed and the flowers will be dry and, although brittle, quite usable for creating your own version of a Victorian pressed-flower picture, as charming and colorful a composition as any valentine you could make. Ideal "flat" flowers for pressing include pansy and viola, hydrangea, daisy, nigella, phlox, delphinium, even nasturtium, and of course, single roses, jasmine, and all manner of cat mints, salvia, and grasses in great variety. This makes a great project for the summer holiday crowd.

ABOVE: To make a very simple bouquet, use the tied bunch method. Gather some special flowers—here, freesia, rosebuds, and hydrangea—in a natural style and bind firmly with raffia or string as you add each flower. Finish with a collar of ivy leaves and add a pretty bow. Voilà!

Index

Reputable Mail-Order Sources

Kurt Bluemel, Inc.
2740 Greene Lane
Baldwin, MD 21013-9523
Phone: (301) 557-7229
Fax: (410) 557-9785
Web site:
www.bluemel.com/kbi/
E-mail: KBI@bluemel.com
*Perennials and extensive list of
ornamental grasses*

Brent & Becky's Bulbs
7463 Health Trail
Gloucester, VA 23061
Web site: www.brentand-
beckysbulbs.com
Phone: (877) 661-2852
*Exciting source of a
full selection of bulbs*

W. Atlee Burpee &
Company
300 Park Avenue
Warminster, PA 18974
Phone: (800) 888-1447
Fax: (215) 674-4170
Web site: www.burpee.
garden.com
*More than seeds, this gardening
fixture also sells plants, bulbs,
and tools*

Gardener's Eden
P.O. Box 7307
San Francisco, CA 94120-
7307
Phone: (800) 822-9600
*Colorful catalog with furniture,
tools, and arranging supplies*

Gardener's Supply Company
128 Intervale Road
Burlington, VT 05401
Phone: (800) 955-3370
Fax: (800) 551-6712
Web site:
www.gardeners.com
E-mail: info@gardeners.com
*Ornaments, supplies, tools,
and everything else*

Heronswood Nursery Ltd.
7530 NE 288th Street
Kingston, WA 98346
Phone: (360) 297-4172
Fax: (360) 297-8321
E-mail:
heronswood@silverlink.net
*This catalog will blow you
away—it's incredible. For the
serious gardener*

Klehm Nursery
4210 North Duncan Road
Champaign, IL 61821
Phone: (800) 553-3715
Fax: (800) 373-8403
Web site: www.klehm.com
E-mail: Klehm@soltc.net
*Peony, hosta, grasses, day lilies,
perennials, and flowering shrubs*

Lilypons Water Gardens
P.O. Box 10
Buckeystown, MD 21717
Phone: (800) 999-5459
Fax: (301) 874-2325
Web site: www.lilypons.com
Water lilies, supplies

McClure & Zimmerman
Phone: (800) 883-6998
Fax: (800) 692-5864
Web site: www.mzbulb.com
E-mail: info@mzbulb.com
Bulbs

Milaeger's Garden Mart, Inc.
4838 Douglas Avenue
Racine, WI 53402
Phone: (800) 669-9956
Fax: (414) 639-1855
Broad selection of perennials

Niche Gardens
111 Dawson Road
Chapel Hill, NC 27516
E-mail:
Mail@nichegdn.com
Phone: (919) 967-0078
Fax: (919) 967-4026
*Expect the unexpected from this
source*

Park Seed Company, Inc.
1 Parkton Avenue
Greenwood, SC 29647
Phone: (800) 845-3369
Fax: (864) 941-4502
Web site:
www.parkseed.com
*Huge selection of plants, seeds,
bulbs, supplies, and tools*

Plant Delights Nurseries Inc.
9241 Sauls Road
Raleigh, NC 27603
E-mail: office@plantdel.com
Phone: (919) 772-4494
Fax: (919) 662-0370
*Special source for the rare
and unusual*

Siskiyou Rare Plant Nursery
2825 Cummings Road
Medford, OR 97501
Phone: (541) 772-6846
Fax: (541) 772-4917
Web site:
www.wavenet/upg/srpn
*Alpine plants, Pacific Northwest
natives, ferns and perennials for
woodland and rock gardens*

Smith & Hawken, Ltd.
2 Arbor Lane
Box 6900
Florence, KY 41022-6900
Phone: (800) 776-3336
Web site:
www.smith.hawken.com
*Tools, furniture, and gardening
gear, including British wellies*

Thompson & Morgan
P.O. Box 1308
Jackson, NJ 08527-0308
Phone: (800) 274-7333
Fax: (908) 363-9356
Web site: www.thompson-
morgan.com
*A famous seed company with
international affiliation*

Wayside Gardens
1 Garden Lane
Hodges, SC 29695-0001
Phone: (800) 845-1124
Fax: (800) 457-9712
Web site:
www.waysidegardens.com
*Roses, perennials, flowering
shrubs, and trees*

We-Du Nurseries
P.O. Box 724 (Route 5)
Marion, NC 28752-93338
Fax: (704) 738-8131
E-mail: wedu@wnclink.com
*Wonderful rock garden
and woodland plants*

White Flower Farm
P.O. Box 50 (Route 63)
Litchfield, CT 06759-0050
Phone: (800) 411-6159
Fax: (800) 496-1418
Web site:
www.whiteflowerfarm.com
*Spring and summer flowering
bulbs, perennials, supplies*

Winterthur Museum
Route 52
Wilmington, DE 19735
Phone: (302) 888-4714
Web site:
www.winterthurgifts.com
*Interesting catalog of
garden-related items plus plants*

Botanical and Plant Societies

Each organization listed can provide much useful information for flower lovers. I recommend membership in the following societies.

American Horticultural Society
P.O. Box 0105
Mount Vernon, VA 22121
Web site: www.ahs.org
Phone: (703) 768-5700

American Rock Garden Society
Exec. Sec. Jaques Mommens
P.O. Box 67
Millwood, NY 10546
E-mail: emommens@IBM.net
Phone: (914) 762-2948

Arnold Arboretum
125 Arborway
Jamaica Plain, MA 02130
Web site: www.arboretum.harvard.edu
Phone: (617) 524-1718
Fax: (617) 524-1418

ARS, The National Arboretum
3501 New York Avenue, NE
Washington, DC 20002
Phone: (202) 245-2726

Brooklyn Botanic Garden
1000 Washington Avenue
Brooklyn, NY 11225
Web site: www.bbg.org
Phone: (718) 623-7200

Chicago Botanic Garden
1000 Lake Cook Road
Glencoe, IL 60022
Web site: www.chicago-botanic.org
Phone: (847) 835-5440
Fax: (847) 835-4484

Garden Club of America
598 Madison Avenue
New York, NY 10022
Web site: www.gcamerica.org
Phone: (212) 753-8287
Local chapters across the United States

Holden Arboretum
9500 Sperry Road
Kirtland, OH 44094-5172
Web site: www.holdenarb.org
Phone: (440) 256-1110

Longwood Gardens
P.O. Box 501
Kennett Square, PA 19348
Phone: (610) 388-1000

Missouri Botanical Garden
P.O. Box 299
St. Louis, MO 63166
Web site: www.mobot.com
Phone: (314) 577-5100
Fax: (314) 577-9595

New England Wildflower Society
Garden in the Woods
Hemenway Road
Framingham, MA 01701
Web site: www.newfs.org
E-mail: newfs@newfs.org
Phone: (508) 877-7630

New York Botanical Garden
Bronx, NY 10458
Phone: (717) 817-8705

Royal Horticultural Society
P.O. Box 313
80 Vincent Square
London SW1P 2PE, England
Web site: www.rhs.org.UK
Phone: (44) 020-7821-3000

Scott Arboretum at Swarthmore College
500 College Avenue
Swarthmore, PA 19081
Phone: (610) 328-8025

Wave Hill
675 West 252nd Street
Bronx, NY 10471
Web site: www.wavchill.org
Phone: (718) 549-3200
Fax: (718) 884-8952

Recommended Reading Lists

The following books are some of the best in the field and have been a great help to me. Some of them may be out of print, but should be available at your local public library or second-hand bookshop.

Austin, David. *The Heritage of the Rose*. London: Antique Collectors Club, 1988.

Berrall, Julia. *The History of Flower Arranging*. New York: Viking Press, 1978.

Blunt, Wilfrid. *The Art of Botanical Illustration*. London: Collins, 1971.

Coates, Peter. *Flowers in History*. New York: Viking Press, 1970.

Dunthorne, Gordon. *Flower and Fruit Prints of the Eighteenth and Early Nineteenth Centuries*. Reprint of the 1938 edition. Washington, D.C.: DaCapo Press, 1970.

Ekstrom, Nicholas, and Ruth R. Clausen. *Perennials for American Gardens*. New York: Random House, 1989.

Everett, Thomas H. *The New York Botanical Garden Illustrated Encyclopedia of Horticulture*. New York: Garland Publishing, 1981.

Harper, Pamela, and Fred McGourty. *Perennials: How to Select, Grow, and Enjoy*. Tucson, Ariz.: HP Books, 1985.

Page, Russell. *The Education of a Gardener*. New York: Random House, 1985.

Turner, Kenneth. *Flower Style*. New York: Weidenfeld and Nicholson, 1989.

Verey, Rosemary. *The Flower Arrangers Garden*. Boston: Little, Brown & Company, 1989.

———. *The Scented Garden*. New York: Van Nostrand Reinhold, 1983.

Photography Credits

Principal photographer: Joseph Mehling
Additional photography: Horst

The photographs that appear on the following pages have been provided by other individuals:

pp. 12–13: Fritz von der Schulenburg
p. 62: J. Barry Ferguson
pp. 78–79: Johann Meier
p. 113: J. Barry Ferguson
p. 112, top: Elizabeth Bilhardt
p. 152: J. Barry Ferguson
p. 153: Johann Meier